"*Rewriting Your Emotional Script* is a book that will produce transformational change in the lives of readers. Becky Harling has skillfully outlined biblical action steps for eliminating mental barriers caused by negative events of the past. This book will give you the tools needed to walk free of guilt and shame into a productive and joy-filled future. It will be invaluable to readers who have experienced heartbreaking mental and physical abuse, but it also belongs in the libraries of all Christian leaders who minister to people who need to let go of past hurts and embrace new beginnings."

—CAROL KENT, speaker;
author of *When I Lay My Isaac Down* and *A New Kind of Normal*

"As Becky has obediently responded to God's whisper to share her story and His message of forgiveness, she has seen the Spirit of God move in mighty ways. His Spirit is gently but powerfully calling women to release their hurts and bitterness to Him. God has unleashed His Spirit in ways she never could have imagined. In this book, Becky shares her desperation and leads us through practical steps of processing our pain, praying Scripture to internalize God's healing truth, and transforming our lives through the renewal of our minds."

—LORRIE LINDGREN, CEO / president, Women of the Harvest,
National Women's Ministries Leadership Team for the EFCA

"This book speaks directly to a woman's heart. Becky gives women a process to rewrite their emotional scripts and let Jesus Christ bind up their broken hearts through the Beatitudes. *Rewriting your Emotional Script* will minister to every woman who is hurting and the study guide makes it a valuable resource for women's Bible studies and small groups."

—JUDY DUNAGAN, director of women's ministries,
Woodmen Valley Chapel, Colorado Springs, Colorado

"Are Christian leaders authentic? Becky Harling is! Are pastors' wives vunerable? Becky Harling is! *Rewriting Your Emotional Script* is a drink of refreshing water for your soul. Read it! You will be changed!"

—LINDA DILLOW, speaker;
author of *Calm My Anxious Heart* and *Satisfy My Thirsty Soul*

DOWNLOAD
A FREE LEADER'S GUIDE AT
www.NavPress.com/emotionalscript

REWRITING YOUR EMOTIONAL SCRIPT

ERASE OLD MESSAGES, EMBRACE NEW ATTITUDES

BECKY HARLING

NAVPRESS

Discipleship Inside Out™

Discipleship Inside Out™

NavPress is the publishing ministry of The Navigators, an international Christian organization and leader in personal spiritual development. NavPress is committed to helping people grow spiritually and enjoy lives of meaning and hope through personal and group resources that are biblically rooted, culturally relevant, and highly practical.

For a free catalog go to www.NavPress.com
or call 1.800.366.7788 in the United States or 1.800.839.4769 in Canada.

ISBN-13: 978-1-60006-188-2

Cover design by www.studiogearbox.com
Cover image by Blaise Hayword/Getty
Creative Team: Kris Wallen, Liz Heaney, Darla Hightower, Linda Vixie, Arvid Wallen, Kathy Guist

All the stories in this book have been used with verbal permission. Unless the individual requested otherwise all the names and some details of each story have been changed to protect privacy. Some of the anecdotal illustrations in this book are true to life and are included with the permission of the persons involved. All other illustrations are composites of real situations, and any resemblance to people living or dead is coincidental.

Unless otherwise identified, all Scripture quotations in this publication are taken from the HOLY BIBLE: NEW INTERNATIONAL VERSION* (NIV*). Copyright © 1973, 1978, 1984 by International Bible Society. Used by permission of Zondervan Publishing House. All rights reserved. Other versions used include: *The New Testament in Modern English* (PH), J. B. Phillips Translator, © J. B. Phillips 1958, 1960, 1972, used by permission of Macmillan Publishing Company; the *New King James Version* (NKJV). Copyright © 1982 by Thomas Nelson, Inc. Used by permission. All rights reserved; the *Holy Bible, New Living Translation* (NLT), copyright © 1996, 2004. Used by permission of Tyndale House Publishers, Inc., Carol Stream, Illinois 60188. All rights reserved; and the *King James Version* (KJV).

Library of Congress Cataloging-in-Publication Data

Harling, Becky, 1957-
  Rewriting your emotional script : erase old messages, embrace new attitudes / Becky Harling.
      p. cm.
  Includes bibliographical references.
  ISBN-13: 978-1-60006-188-2
  ISBN-10: 1-60006-188-5
  1. Beatitudes--Criticism, interpretation, etc. 2. Emotions--Religious aspects--Christianity. 3. Christian women--Religious life. I. Title.
  BT382.H27 2008
  248.8'43--dc22

                                    2008006484

Printed in the United States of America

3 4 5 6 7 8 9 / 14 13 12 11 10

This book is lovingly dedicated to

Jesus Christ, my Holy Healer.

I praise You for redeeming my life from the pit.

And to

Kris Hungerford, a healer after God's heart.

You have taught me how to rewrite my emotional script.

I love you and will be forever grateful!

CONTENTS

ACKNOWLEDGMENTS

S pecial thanks to:

My husband, Steve: In many ways we rewrote our emotional scripts together. Thank you for believing I could do it, and for loving me in the journey. Oh, how I love you!

My amazing children:

Bethany, God is using your gentleness in many lives. Thank you for all the times you listened as I processed the ideas taught in this book with you! God is already using you to help others rewrite their emotional scripts. I love you!

Josiah, your strength and wisdom are gifts from God. Your encouragement has proved invaluable to me as I have written this book. I love you, my son!

Stefanie, your passion for God will someday change the world. Thank you for helping me with the chapter about becoming hungry for God. I love you!

Keri Joy, your compassion amazes and inspires me. God is using you in the lives of so many of your friends. You have helped me rewrite my emotional script — especially in the area of mercy. I love you!

My son-in-law, Dave Holder: I love your heart for God. Thanks for all the times we hung out last summer talking about this book.

My precious mentor, Linda Dillow: Thank you for walking with me through the journey as I worked to rewrite my emotional script. I love you!

My dear friends Jill and Judy: You have prayed me through this book. All the times when I wanted to quit you held up my arms through prayer. I love you both!

My incredible editor, Liz Heaney: Wow. You are truly amazing! Thank you for believing I could do this, even when I didn't think I could. Your wisdom and encouragement throughout this project have been remarkable. I could have never done it without you.

The precious women at Foothills Community Church: Thank you for welcoming and embracing me. We've known each other only a short while, but I love you already. Thank you to all of you who field-tested this book. I love each one of you!

The wonderful team at NavPress: What a privilege to be published by you. Special thanks to Kris Wallen for all your encouragement throughout this project.

NOTE TO SMALL GROUP LEADERS

I believe God is going to use you in ways you cannot imagine as you use this book to help women rewrite their emotional scripts. You will become a curate. "The word curate signifies a person who partners with God for the 'cure of the soul.'"[1] It's essential that you do everything possible to provide a safe environment for group members. Please discourage any advice giving, unless the member asks specifically for advice, and insist on confidentiality. Have a list of godly, well-trained therapists to whom you can refer members of your group who need additional support. Above all else, pray for the members of your group by name. I believe with all my heart that you are going to watch the Lord perform mighty works of healing in the lives of your group members as you partner with Him!

CHAPTER 1

THIS WASN'T SUPPOSED TO BE MY STORY!

A s I lay on the hotel bed in tears, I prayed, *Lord Jesus, please. This wasn't supposed to be my story! If there's any other message, I will give it! How could You use something so messy . . . so . . . ugly?*

I was in Eastern Europe to minister to about fifteen hundred women who would momentarily fill the conference room to hear of God's redemptive love. And I was a mess. It was the opening night, and I was to give a brief testimony about God's grace in my life. Sounds simple enough . . . unless your story includes childhood sexual abuse.

All I'd ever wanted to be was a Bible teacher, to give women Jesus. While I had many of the signs of one who had been sexually abused, the memories didn't resurface until well into my adult life. Trust me, I didn't go looking for them. Through a series of divinely orchestrated traumatic events, breast cancer and subsequent surgeries included, God allowed the memories to resurface.

Now He was calling me to tell others about the ugliest part of my life, and the prospect filled me with fear. As I entered the ballroom where I was to speak, old messages flooded my mind: "Don't tell. Don't tell. Don't tell." My throat felt so tight, I wondered if I could get any words out. Silently, I told myself, "Keep breathing, deep breaths. Don't pass out." *Holy One, help me!*

Somehow I made it through that night. I don't remember what I said, but I know that as I accepted the microphone, I heard the Holy Spirit's faint whisper, "Becky, give Me your story. It's not horrible. In fact, it's a story of hope and healing."

While I can't change my story, I can rewrite the script that directs my life. Let me explain.

The Lens Through Which We View Life

For the last ten years I've been on a journey to manage my feelings and change my perspective. It hasn't been easy. The sexual abuse I experienced as a child left an indelible mark on me. As a result, my emotional script was full of shame, insecurity, guilt, low self-esteem, anger, and fear. I felt sad and lonely and constantly wondered what was wrong with me. When someone betrayed me, the hurt felt like a devastating blow to the core of who I was, leaving me stunned and often unable to think clearly. I would withdraw from the relationship rather than work through the hard stuff, because the hard stuff hurt too much. When my feelings began to overwhelm me, I coped by resorting to control, defensiveness, mistrust, and pride, because I didn't know what else to do. I taught myself how to live as a performer, pretending I had life all together.

In the beginning, I wanted to revise my emotional script because I didn't want to be a victim. Victims feel as though life has dealt them an unfair blow, and they are unable or unwilling to move past the hurt. As a result they not only suffer, but their families suffer as well. I did not want to do that to my husband and my children.

I so want the script I live out to be in line with what God has for me, instead of the hodgepodge of truth and lies that used to dictate my thoughts and behavior. When my heart aches, for whatever reason, I want my feelings and reactions to reflect my true identity as God's child. Don't you? That's why I determined to rewrite the emotional script I had followed for so many years. I needed to erase the old messages and replace them with new attitudes.

Each of us is born with a unique, God-given personality that forms the basis of our emotional scripts—the lens through which each of us views life. The thought patterns and attitudes that flow out of our scripts often dictate our responses and reactions.

However, as we grow up,

> *Our original, God-given emotional scripts*
> *are often warped by the messages that our*
> *experiences, our circumstances, and the voices*
> *of significant people wrote on our hearts.*
> *These scripts become the screenplays for our*
> *lives, dictating our responses and reactions.*

Some of those messages are true, some are false. The problem is that as children we do not have the capability to edit those messages, so we absorb them *all* as truth. As a result, our emotional scripts are skewed.

Skewed Scripts

For example, I was born with a passionate and expressive personality. I feel things deeply and express my emotions openly. This is who God created me to be. However, as I child I didn't understand this. So when I heard over and over again, "Becky, stop crying. You're too sensitive. Why do you make such a big deal out of everything?" I began to think something was wrong with me. These and similar comments skewed my emotional script by imprinting it with false messages that said I was overly sensitive and blew things out of proportion. Consequently, whenever I cried as an adult, I felt guilty, ashamed, and embarrassed.

Beth grew up in an extremely dysfunctional family. Her father continually called her vile names, and her mother told her that she would never amount to anything. Those words were branded on Beth's mind and heart at a very young age, and consequently her emotional script was full of negative thoughts about who she was.

My friend Mimi, the daughter of missionary parents, attended boarding school. She struggled with a learning disability, and when her teachers repeatedly told her she was stupid, Mimi believed them. After all, missionaries are supposed to be godly, so weren't they telling her the truth? Consequently, Mimi's emotional script caused her to doubt her intellectual abilities.

Although God designed our original emotional scripts and we bear His image, sin has radically altered our scripts. Each of us was born into a sinful world with sinful parents, grandparents, and neighbors. At some point, all of us have experienced hurt and disappointment, and in our effort to survive, we have internalized harmful messages about ourselves and the world that overwhelm us when we feel threatened. These messages often dictate our actions.

Please understand that I am *not* saying it's wrong or sinful to feel angry or depressed or afraid. Feelings, in and of themselves, are not wrong. How we feel is just how we feel. In fact, God created our emotions and is emotional Himself. For example, He feels joy (Luke 10:21), anger (Matthew 21:12-17), grief and sorrow (John 11:33-35), and sadness (Mark 14:34). We will experience hurt, fear, and anger. However, they must be managed or they can run wild, tempting us to believe things that aren't true — *My life is hopeless. Nothing will ever change. I'm stupid and unimportant. No one cares about me. I always flub it, so why even try?* When we believe such lies,

- We may decide to never trust again. After all, it feels horrible to hurt so deeply. So we build protective walls that insulate us from ever feeling that ripping pain again.
- We may lash out in revenge. When Sheila found out her husband had been having an affair for over ten years, she became so angry she charged $22,000 on his credit card.

- We may choose bitterness. In the process of rehearsing the pain over and over, our hearts slowly turn to stone. If we choose this option, we leave a legacy of bitterness. One author wrote, "Bitterness is like a rock thrown into a placid pond; after its initial splash, it sends out concentric circles that disturb the whole pond. It starts with ourselves, expands to our spouse, then to our children, friends and colleagues."[1]
- We may become angry and withdraw from God. After all, He could have protected us, but chose not to. Doesn't this give us the right to blame Him?
- We may succumb to hopelessness and spend the rest of our lives anesthetizing our pain through various addictions.

But avoidance of painful truth only makes us run harder and faster in an effort to deny the obvious. After a time the illusion will crash. But it doesn't have to be this way. We can rewrite our emotional scripts.

REVISING OUR SCRIPTS WITH GOD'S LIFE-GIVING ATTITUDES

The apostle Paul wrote to the believers in Rome and instructed them that their attitudes were critical to their spiritual development: "Those who live according to the sinful nature have their minds set on what that nature desires; but those who live in accordance with the Spirit have their minds set on what the Spirit desires" (Romans 8:5). The Greek word translated *mind* in this passage, *phronema*, means a "way of thinking" or a "mindset."[2] Paul went on to say that this mindset is to be made new (Romans 12:1-2).

Our mindsets are a collection of thoughts and attitudes that have become habitual. Rewriting our emotional scripts will mean erasing old messages that are harmful and replacing them with new messages, new attitudes. In essence, we are changing our emotional patterns or responses.

Our minds choose what we dwell on and for how long. For example, if I choose to think about all the things that I am concerned might go wrong when I send my child off to college, my fears can intensify and overwhelm me. But if every time I have an anxious thought I think instead about the sovereignty of God and about how much He loves my child, then I am giving the Holy Spirit the opportunity to transform me.

Erwin Lutzer, former senior pastor of The Moody Church, wrote, "I believe that the transformation of our attitudes is the key to seeing the world through the eyes of faith; it is the key to the inner work of the Holy Spirit in our lives."[3] The only way this transformation is possible is if we first exchange the negative messages in our emotional scripts with God's life-giving attitudes. Then the Holy Spirit can do the inner work of emotional and spiritual transformation; as we rewrite our thought patterns, He can give us an attitude makeover.

My determination to rewrite my script led me to study what the Bible says about Jesus. In His Sermon on the Mount, I found the answers I was looking for. Six times throughout this sermon Jesus said, "You have heard that it was said . . . but I tell you" (Matthew 5:21-22,27-28,31-32,33-34,38-39,43-44). In other words, don't believe the messages of the past. Instead, rewrite the script and choose the attitudes of the kingdom.

Many people in the crowds that gathered to hear Jesus speak were broken, wounded, hurting, lonely, and afraid. Seated on the picturesque mountainside in Palestine, He offered hope to the hurting. In the Sermon on the Mount we find insight for how we can rewrite our emotional scripts so that they are both healthy and holy. Read it for yourself:

> *Blessed are the poor in spirit,*
> *for theirs is the kingdom of heaven.*

Blessed are those who mourn,
for they will be comforted.

Blessed are the meek,
for they will inherit the earth.

Blessed are those who hunger and thirst for righteousness,
for they will be filled.

Blessed are the merciful,
for they will be shown mercy.

Blessed are the pure in heart,
for they will see God.

Blessed are the peacemakers,
for they will be called sons of God.

Blessed are those who are persecuted because of righteousness,
for theirs is the kingdom of heaven.

Blessed are you when people insult you, persecute you and falsely
say all kinds of evil against you because of me. Rejoice and be glad,
because great is your reward in heaven. (Matthew 5:2-12)

I believe that each beatitude can be a stepping-stone toward rewriting our emotional scripts. The transformation does not happen quickly. In fact, I have come to realize that there are messages in my emotional script that need to be erased every day for me to embrace these new attitudes. The rewriting is an ongoing, lifelong process, not a one-time transaction. In many ways it is like peeling an onion. God peels back a layer, revealing a negative message written on our scripts and our sinful response to that message. We confess that sinful response, erase the lie, replace it with truth, and choose a godly attitude. God then peels back another layer and reveals another negative message and so on until our entire scripts are revised. This rewriting of our scripts takes a lifetime.

However, we don't have to wait until the end to see change. Each beatitude offers transformation in and of itself. While we don't change ourselves (that's the Holy Spirit's job), as we cooperate with Him by choosing these attitudes, we open our hearts for Him to make us more like the people we were created to be.

I wish I could tell you that I am completely emotionally healthy and spiritually mature after having gone through these steps. But that would be a lie, and I am committed to authenticity. What I can tell you is that by adopting these attitudes, I am further on the journey than I was a few years ago, and I am committed to replacing the destructive and sinful parts of my emotional script with the life-giving attitudes found in the Beatitudes. Every time I get hurt I am given a new opportunity to embrace these attitudes. Gradually, the Holy Spirit is pouring hope and strength into this fragile heart.

How to Use This Book

I want to take you on a journey to rewrite your emotional script as I have done. The promise of change lies ahead! Throughout the rest of this book, we are going to study and examine each of the Beatitudes in depth. At the end of each chapter is a section called "Praying Scripture to Internalize Truth." The Scriptures are God's words found in the Bible. And because they are *God's* words, they are powerful! When we pray them back to God, we invite His power into our pain. You see, even after we have erased old messages, replaced them with truth, and chosen new attitudes, it's easy to forget our commitment. God's Word is "living and active." It is "sharper than any double-edged sword[;] it penetrates even to dividing soul and spirit" (Hebrews 4:12). In other words, the verses are able to transform not only our conscious minds but even our subconscious thoughts. When we pray God's Word, we raise the power of this double-edged sword over our emotional scripts. God's Spirit then uses that sword to heal and change the damaged parts of our emotions. So when you come to the end of the chapter, try praying these Scripture-based prayers. Then try writing prayers of your own, using Bible verses that you know.

Next is a study section called "Further Transformation." I believe it will be most effective if it is completed in a small-group setting. I encourage you to ask a Bible study leader in your church to lead a group, using this book. Or consider forming a group on your own and appointing a leader. However, if being part of a group study is not an option, you will still benefit tremendously by working through this section on your own. I recommend that you find a close friend or mentor with whom you can process the ideas taught in this book.

Each study section has four parts designed to help you as you rewrite your emotional script:

- **Meditating on and memorizing a passage of Scripture.** As you fill your mind with Scripture there will be less room for the old messages.
- **Digging deeper into the Scriptures.** While these questions may be done as an individual they will be most effective discussed within a small group or mentoring setting. Throughout the book we will be discussing the importance of community. I believe that spiritual growth happens most effectively in the context of community. Hebrews reminds, "Let us not give up meeting together" (10:25), "but encourage one another daily, as long as it is called Today, so that none of you may be hardened by sin's deceitfulness" (3:13). James instructs, "Therefore confess your sins to each other and pray for each other so that you may be healed" (5:16).
- **Probing deeper into your personal emotional script.** These questions and spiritual exercises are designed to let

you get in touch with your feelings. They should be done alone and unrushed under the direction of the Holy Spirit. It is possible that while answering these questions some buried issues may surface. Please do not be afraid to seek godly counseling from a well-trained Christian therapist.

- **Unleashing the power of praise.** This is one of the most essential tools you can embrace as you rewrite your emotional script. When you choose to praise God, He pours new hope and joy into your life.

You Can Change!

I have so much confidence in this message that I am willing to make you a promise: *If you implement them, the principles in this book will transform your thinking!* If you follow them and do your part of rewriting, the Holy Spirit will do His part of transforming.

As you seek to erase negative messages and replace them with God's life-changing attitudes, please keep in mind the following principles:

- **Transformation begins with a choice.** One of my favorite verses is found in Colossians 3:16: "Let the Word of Christ dwell in you richly." I love the word *let* in this verse because it reminds me *I have a choice.* The same is true for you.
- **Transformation happens slowly.** Bummer, but true! If you're like me, you want your attitudes transformed quickly. But life-changing transformation happens only as we submit to the indwelling power of the Holy Spirit, facing one hurtful situation after another. This is what Peter was referring to when he wrote about the "sanctifying work of the Spirit" (1 Peter 1:2). Sanctification makes us more like Christ.
- **Transformation happens as we replace old thought patterns with new ones found in Scripture.** You have to want to put your thoughts—instead of your emotions—in

control of what you believe and do. Paul wrote, "Do not conform any longer to the pattern of this world [or to the patterns of thinking set in place over years of time], but [instead] be transformed by the renewing of your mind" (Romans 12:2, bracketed material added). As you *choose* to meditate on Scripture and replace old thoughts with healthier and holier thoughts, the Holy Spirit will transform you.

When people or circumstances hurt or disappoint or threaten you, you can move beyond hurt and fear and respond in ways that lead to joy and life rather than pain and death. I know because I've tested these principles myself. As I've rewritten my emotional script with the attitudes in the Beatitudes, the Holy Spirit is gradually changing me. He will do the same for you.

PRAYING SCRIPTURE
TO INTERNALIZE TRUTH

I worship You, Holy Healer, because You know every intimate detail of my emotional script. You designed and created me. "Lord, you have searched me and you know me." You know every thought and feeling written on my heart. "You know when I sit and when I rise; you perceive my thoughts from afar. You discern my going out and my lying down; you are familiar with all my ways. Before a word is on my tongue you know it completely" (Psalm 139:1-4). Before I was ever born You saw the hurts I would experience. Lord, my emotional script is so complicated. You understand me better than I understand myself. Help me as I begin to rewrite.

Your Word tells me that "all the days ordained for me were written in your book before one of them came to be" (Psalm 139:16). Father, I confess I don't understand Your ways. If I had scripted my life it would not have included _____ (*fill in the blank with the hurtful situation that has been especially difficult for you*). Yet, Holy One, I know You are sovereign. "Search me, O God, and know my heart; test me and know my anxious thoughts" (Psalm 139:23). Reveal to me the coping mechanisms that I have used so often in my desire to run from pain. Show me any offensive or defensive way (see Psalm 139:24).

Lord, uproot denial in me. "If I have walked in falsehood or my foot has hurried after deceit" (Job 31:5), forgive me. Holy Spirit, infuse me with courage to face truthfully the patterns of thinking and attitudes that I have developed over the years. You have said, "There is nothing concealed that will not be disclosed, or hidden that will not be made known" (Luke 12:2). I am resting in Your promise that "you will know the truth, and the truth will set you free" (John 8:32).

"Sovereign Lord, my strong deliverer, who shields my head in the day of battle" (Psalm 140:7), strengthen me as I embark on this journey of rewriting my emotional script. Your desire is that I be set free and conformed to the image of Your Son, Jesus Christ. I praise You that You will be faithful throughout the process.

FURTHER TRANSFORMATION
Digging Deeper into the Scriptures

1. Memorize and meditate on Romans 12:1-2, as written here or in another translation.

   > Therefore, I urge you, brothers, in view of God's mercy, to offer your bodies as living sacrifices, holy and pleasing to God—this is your spiritual act of worship. Do not conform any longer to the pattern of this world, but be transformed by the renewing of your mind.

2. Read through Matthew 5:1-14. Imagine that you are in the crowd, sitting and listening to Jesus. Describe the scene. What do you see, hear, and smell? What are you thinking and feeling as you listen to Jesus' words?

3. In your own words (or as a group) define an emotional script. Write your definition here.

4. Read 2 Corinthians 5:17. Paraphrase the verse in your own words. According to this verse why is rewriting your emotional script so important? Think of a word picture that you feel best describes the life transformation that is to happen to followers of Christ. Describe that word picture here.

5. Read Psalm 139, then answer the following questions:
   a. According to verses 1-3, how well does God know you? Describe His knowledge of you here.

   b. According to verse 7, is it possible to hide from God? What impact does this verse have on patterns of denial you may have developed?

   c. According to verses 13-15, we are to praise God for how He has designed us and the events He has allowed in our lives. Is this hard for you? Why or why not?

d. Write your own paraphrase of verses 23-24, asking God to help you understand what is written on your emotional script.

6. The process of rewriting your emotional script involves both you and God.

a. Describe your part:

b. Describe God's part:

Probing Deeper into Your Emotional Script

7. Get alone with God. On a piece of paper draw a timeline of your life. Include on your timeline three traumatic events that shaped your emotional script. Journal about those three events in the space provided below.

8. Write a summary of your emotional script in the space below. Underline the messages in your emotional script that you would like to see changed. Identify which of those messages are lies. For example:

Lies

I am damaged goods.
I am worthless unless I perform.

9. Choose three specific areas of your emotional script that you would like to see transformed as a result of this study. Think in terms of attitudes. Journal about each of those areas here.

a.

b.

c.

10. Read Romans 8:29. According to this verse, we are to be "conformed" to the likeness of Jesus. Look back over the three areas that you just listed as parts of your emotional script that you would like to see changed. If these three attitudes were changed, how would you be more like Jesus?

11. Write a prayer to the Lord, describing to Him your hopes for this Bible study.

12. Unleash the power of praise. Psalm 150 (page 30) gives some great suggestions on how to praise God. Read the psalm and allow it to prompt your praise. Spend time praising God for whatever comes to your mind.

Praise the LORD.
Praise God in his sanctuary;
 praise him in his mighty heavens.
Praise him for his acts of power;
 praise him for his surpassing greatness.
Praise him with the sounding of the trumpet,
 praise him with the harp and lyre,
praise him with the tambourine and dancing,
 praise him with the strings and flute,
praise him with the clash of cymbals,
 praise him with resounding cymbals.
Let everything that has breath praise the LORD.
Praise the LORD.

CHAPTER 2

BECOME DESPERATE AND DETERMINED FOR HELP

Blessed are the poor in spirit.

MATTHEW 5:3

One night after I spoke at a retreat, twenty-year-old Gerry came up to me and fell into my arms, sobbing. I stroked her hair and held her, silently asking God for wisdom for how to help and comfort her. When her tears subsided, Gerry poured out her story.

Her father was put in jail when Gerry was only four years old. She felt very ashamed and, like many children who have parents in jail, blamed herself, thinking, *If I had been a better little girl my daddy would not have gone to jail.* While Gerry was still a child, her mom became an active lesbian. Embarrassed by her mother's choices, Gerry, prompted by her emotional script, coped by engaging in an all-out campaign to prove she was not like her mother. Gerry's sexual involvement with boys became her ticket to the "in" crowd. Yet she could never shake the painful feelings inside her. Instead of erasing her shame, her promiscuity only compounded it with feelings of guilt.

In an effort to anesthetize the pain she felt inside and perhaps punish herself for her sexual activity, Gerry began to cut herself. Every time she felt overwhelmed with shame or sadness, she made small cuts on her arms. She desperately wanted her shame to go away, to somehow be erased, and she said that the pain from cutting herself brought temporary relief from the pain she felt inside. However, after hearing me speak about the Cross, Gerry told me, "I get it. For the first time, I get it. Jesus was cut so I don't have to cut anymore. By His wounds I am healed."

Even though Gerry's emotional script was deeply flawed, she was exactly where she needed to be for God to transform her. She finally understood that cutting wasn't the answer to her problems. She knew that Christ was the one who could heal her, and she was determined to seek Him and His help.

Gerry was right. We can't fix ourselves. Rather than pulling out the coping mechanisms written into our emotional scripts—denial, anger, avoidance, addictions, and so on—we need to do something radically different. Jesus calls His followers to courageously face their mess and embrace their brokenness. He said, "Blessed are the poor in spirit" (Matthew 5:3). Every person who wants to rewrite her emotional script must begin here.

What It Means to Be "Poor in Spirit"

The Greek word translated here as *poor, plocho,* is derived from a root that means "crouch." *Plocho* suggests a beggar who kneels at the feet of others in hopes that they will supply her needs.[1] In the early 1980s we lived in Sudan during that country's civil war, and I saw many broken, mangled beggars sitting on their haunches, desperately looking up for financial help. Their only hope was a handout from others, and they knew it. In this beatitude Jesus is encouraging us to have the same attitude as those beggars. He wants us to be empty of self, to be so focused on our need for help that we don't worry about what others think or how we might look. He wants us to be desperate and determined for Him.

TO BECOME POOR IN SPIRIT MEANS:

I recognize my need for God.
In my desperation, I cry out for help.
I determine to pursue Him as my only hope,
both for forgiveness of sins and for emotional healing.

How desperate for God are you? Too many Christians believe that to "be spiritual" means not having any problems, not burdening others with our "stuff." This is nonsense. We all have our "stuff." That is why Jesus came to earth. He said, "It is not the healthy who need a doctor, but the sick. I have not come to call the righteous, but sinners" (Mark 2:17). He came to bind up the wounds of those who are hurting (see Isaiah 61). Throughout His ministry Jesus emphasized that the spiritually mature are those who become like children. Children are the least, and they are desperate for His healing and mercy (see Matthew 18:3-4).

Christ doesn't reserve His kingdom for superheroes. Instead, He came for those who are broken and desperate. He reached down, became poor in spirit Himself, and offered to make us whole. He delights in rescuing those who are hurting and then redeeming our mess for His glory. To some degree or another, all of us are broken inside. You may find yourself constantly insecure in relationships, constantly trying to prove yourself to others, or constantly in competition with them. Or maybe you find yourself fearful of God, filled with guilt and shame because of how despicable you are.

Whatever your area of brokenness, how determined are you to receive God's help? In our desperation we often cry out to counselors and friends. This is good. Godly counselors and friends are helpful. But when we become poor in spirit, we come to recognize that Jesus Christ is our only deliverer, and we determine to know Him better. Others can encourage, but only Jesus Christ can free us from sin and the effects of sin on our emotional scripts.

TWO DESPERATE PEOPLE, TWO NEEDS MET

Two biblical characters from opposite ends of the social spectrum illustrate what it looks like to become poor in spirit: Jairus and the woman with the issue of blood. Both "crouched" before Jesus and recognized Him as their only hope. Let's take a look at their stories in Luke 8:40-56.

Jairus held a prominent position in the local synagogue. Powerful and successful, he had every reason to feel proud of his accomplishments. After all, he had his life together. Then his little girl became deathly ill, and none of that mattered anymore. When Jairus realized that she was not getting better and would most likely die, he ran in search of Jesus, the miracle worker. When he found Him, he fell at His feet and pleaded with Jesus to come to his house and heal his daughter. Jesus readily agreed, and they set off for Jairus's house.

Following close behind them was a woman also desperate for Jesus. She had been bleeding for twelve years. According to Old Testament law, a woman who was experiencing her monthly flow was considered unclean and was forbidden to enter the synagogue, even to worship. Not only was this woman sick, she was likely poor because her illness would have made her an outcast, abandoned by her family and friends. Imagine the shame of being considered "unclean" for twelve years!

This woman had heard about the miracles Jesus had performed, and she was determined to find Him so that He could heal her. She was likely familiar with the teaching of the prophets and knew that the prophet Malachi had prophesied that when the promised Messiah came, He would rise with healing in His wings (see Malachi 4:2). The word translated as *wings* here is the Hebrew word *kanaf. Kanaf* can also be translated *corners.*[2] That's important, because in the book of Numbers, God told His people that they were to attach tassels to the corners of their garments (see Numbers 15:38-40). These tassels were to be a visual reminder of God's goodness and loving-kindness, as well as a reminder of His commands. It is conceivable that Jesus, being a Jew, had these tassels sewn into the corners of the hem of His robe.

From what she had heard about Jesus, the woman believed Him to be the Messiah, and she was watching and waiting for just the right opportunity to touch His robe so that she could be healed. She had gone from doctor to doctor, and none of them had helped her. Her money was gone and her hope fragile. In a courageous act of faith, she grabbed hold of Jesus' tassels. Instantly, the flow of blood stopped and her illness was cured.

Jesus felt the release of His healing power and turned, asking, "Who touched me?" The disciples were incredulous and Peter reminded Jesus that the crowds had been pressing in on Him the whole time He'd been walking. I wonder if Jesus thought, *Well, thank you very much, Peter. I wonder how I survived all those years before I created you!* Jesus knew that someone had just experienced a major miracle. He turned and searched the crowd with compassionate eyes.

Trembling with fear, the woman came forward and told Him her story. Can you imagine talking about your menstrual problems in front of the disciples, not to mention the crowd? I imagine the disciples were probably thinking, *Does she have to talk about* that? Meanwhile, Jairus was waiting. The clock was ticking. Time was running out. His daughter was dying. He was about to lose his *only* daughter, and this woman was pouring out her heart about her hormones! Imagine what was going through his mind.

Only after listening to her story did Jesus continue on with Jairus to his house, but before they arrived a messenger came and told Jairus that his daughter had already died. Jesus continued on to Jairus's house, and instead of healing his daughter, He raised her from the dead. Gently, He bent over her bed and whispered, "My child, get up!" (Luke 8:54). It is as if Jesus says, "My beloved little girl, wake up!" I love that phrase! It reminds me of just how tenderly Jesus speaks to us. There comes a times in each of our lives when He tenderly says, "My beloved little girl, wake up — wake up and face the truth about what's written on your emotional script." This is what He did for me. He gently bent down and said, "Beloved Becky, my precious child, wake up. Now's the time to face the memories." As I faced those memories and rewrote my script, He brought new life to my soul.

Before we leave this story, let me ask you a question about the woman. Why would Jesus put her through the humiliation of telling Him her story in front of the crowd? How embarrassing! He could have preserved her dignity and just let her sneak away quietly. But He didn't. While we can't know for sure because Scripture doesn't tell us, I can think of several reasons why Jesus may have put this woman on the spot.

First, He placed a high value on community. He never meant for us to walk our spiritual journeys alone, in isolation. It's entirely conceivable that other women in the crowd had experienced the same problem this woman had. Perhaps they would be able to offer her encouragement. Perhaps they would even find hope themselves. This woman had felt isolated and lonely for twelve years, without fellowship in her local synagogues. For her to rewrite her emotional script, she probably needed other women to rally around her.

Second, I believe that Jesus wanted to publicly free this woman from shame. In making a public statement about her healing, He ensured that the local Jewish leaders would allow her to once again participate in corporate worship. His public statement of her healing would set her free from the shame of being declared ceremonially unclean. Because of Jewish law, her emotional script had read "unclean." Because of Christ's healing, her new script read "clean."

I find in this story tremendous hope for every woman who is hurting or feeling as if her heart is bleeding. Jesus cares about your pain. If you will come to Him desperate and determined, He will heal the broken places of your heart. I know, because one morning I bowed low before Him and prayed, *Lord, I will cling to the corner of Your robe and hold on for dear life. Even if You drag me on my face through the dirt, I will not let go!* God honored both my desperation and my determination. He brought healing and wholeness to my life, and He can do the same for you.

May I ask you, do you need healing? Is there something about your responses to life and people that you would like to change? Jesus cares about every hurt in your life. He wants you to experience His presence and He longs for you to find wholeness. But for that to happen, you must be desperate for His help. Are you? If not, you may need to remove the barriers of pride and shame so that you can become poor in spirit.

The Barriers to Poverty of Spirit

Both of these emotions take our eyes off of Christ and lead us to an unhealthy preoccupation with self.

Pride says, "I want people to think I have my life together." Pride makes us feel foolish about bowing before a God we cannot see. Pride makes us feel embarrassed about crying to God for help, because it says we should be able to come up with a solution ourselves. Pride says that even though we don't like our mess and it's too big to clean up, we don't want other people to know about it because they may think less of us.

Shame says, "I am damaged goods. I am too dirty to have a relationship with God. Why would He want me?" Shame is the pervasive sense that we are defective, inadequate, and worthless. Author Cynthia Spell Humbert said, "Shame is the paralyzing emotion in which the afflicted person believes irreparable damage has been done to the deepest part of her soul." She goes on to write, "Shame pushes people to hide their true selves."[3]

Sometimes we feel shame because of sin that others have done to us: They abused us, failed to accept us, criticized us, judged us, betrayed us, and so on. Other times we feel shame because of our own sin. When we sin, we may feel convicted. This is not shame. Conviction calls us to repentance. Shame shouts that we are permanently unacceptable to God, so there's no point in repenting. This is a lie. Those who come to Christ Jesus are never found unacceptable (see Romans 8:1).

Shame is like a pit. It feels dirty, mucky, and hopeless. I've been in that pit, but God rescued me. I can now say with the psalmist David,

"He lifted me out of the slimy pit, out of the mud and mire; he set my feet on a rock and gave me a firm place to stand" (Psalm 40:2). If you are in the pit of shame, God wants you out! Please don't let this barrier prevent you from crying out to Him in desperation. He will hear your cry.

I don't know if pride or shame is a barrier for you, but if so, you can begin tearing down the barrier and rewriting your script. You may be wondering, *How? How do I become "poor in spirit," moment by moment, even when my circumstances aren't desperate?*

Getting in Touch with Desperation

Here are a few questions to ask yourself. These questions are designed to help you get in touch with your need for God. As you take inventory, ask God to develop in you a deep desire for Himself.

1. Do I have any patterns of behavior that I am trying to keep secret? Often, the patterns of behavior that we are trying to keep secret are sinful. The problem is that it generally takes more energy to cover up sin and keep secrets than it does to bring them out in the open and confess them.

I met Betsy at a retreat. She told me about the broken relationships in her life and about the physical abuse she had experienced as a child. I listened quietly for a long time and then I heard the Spirit whispering in my heart, "Ask her what she thinks of Jesus." I silently argued a bit, praying, *Lord, she's at a church retreat. Surely she knows Jesus.* But once again I felt the Spirit's voice prompting me, "Ask her what she thinks of Jesus." So I did.

At first Betsy was caught off guard, but then she hesitantly replied that she didn't really know who Jesus was, so I began to share with her my Jesus. Everything was going fine until we got to the part about each of us being a sinner. Betsy wasn't sure she agreed. Even though she agreed that sin had been committed against her, the only thing she could think of that she had ever done wrong was stealing something as a child.

We talked at length about the continuum of sin. I pointed out that everyone sins, from Mother Teresa to the worst murderer sitting in jail. When I asked Betsy where she was on that continuum, she thought for a long time. Then she began to cry. All of a sudden it hit her that even as an adult she had sinned. She began to tell me about her sexual flings of the previous few years. (She had not told anyone about these affairs.) Even though she had never thought of them as sin, she had kept them secret just the same. Betsy realized she needed to bring her secret sins to Jesus and to ask forgiveness. Together we got down on our knees and Betsy admitted her need. She realized that she could no longer hide her sin, that she needed Jesus.

Even though you may have already put your faith and trust in Jesus, it is possible that you are hiding some secret sin. Often those secrets leave us feeling trapped. That trapped feeling can either prompt us to hide or propel us to confess. Either way, we are unable to break free ourselves. We need Jesus.

If you are not in the habit of confessing your sins, ask the Holy Spirit to search your heart and reveal them to you. David wrote, "Search me, O God, and know my heart; test me and know my anxious thoughts. See if there is any offensive way in me, and lead me in the way everlasting" (Psalm 139:23-24).

2. Do I have any broken or strained relationships? These provide a good clue to other areas of your life that might be hurting. When Patti took inventory of her relationships, the Holy Spirit brought to mind a friend who had hurt her several years before. Since that time there had been distance between them. Patti realized that rather than dealing with conflict, her modus operandi had been to back up and put distance between herself and her friend. The Holy Spirit helped her see that this was unhealthy. She became poor in spirit by approaching her friend and asking if they could start over.

3. Have I believed any lies that are holding me back from all that God has for me? What are the lies written in my emotional script? One common lie women believe is "God cannot use me because of some sin I committed." That's what Lisa believed. Her parents had taught her a lie, saying that it was important for her to experiment sexually during her teen years. (Sex is a beautiful gift that God gave for marriage.) However, when Lisa became pregnant at age sixteen, her mother wrote a different message on Lisa's emotional script. Her mother felt horrified that her daughter was pregnant, so she scheduled an abortion. Mixed messages like these—be promiscuous; don't get pregnant—are what counselors call "crazy making," because they are written by the same person on one script and they present a double bind—a lose-lose situation.

Five or six months after her abortion, Lisa's father became sarcastic and hostile toward her. He began to make comments to Lisa about the mess she had gotten herself into and the cost of her mistake. Those comments became branded on her emotional script, compounding her feelings of guilt and shame. In an effort to relieve her guilt, Lisa began to purge (forcing herself to throw up after meals), internalizing another lie, "I can cleanse myself." It wasn't long until her eating disorder controlled Lisa's life. In desperation, she cried out for help and checked into an eating-disorder clinic. There she met a Christian counselor who began to help her understand the lies written on her script. But even after Lisa began to rewrite her script, one big lie remained—"God cannot use me because of the abortion." Fear tormented Lisa for many years, even after she married a godly man. She feared God would punish her by never allowing her to get pregnant again. After all, how could God ever trust her to raise a child after the sin she had committed? It took several years of peeling back layers with the Christian counselor before Lisa began to internalize the truth that because she had repented, God had forgiven her. She eventually gave birth to three beautiful children, and God used and continues to use her story to change many lives.

4. Do any of my emotional responses feel like an overreaction? Or do others close to me see my responses as an overreaction? If so, can I identify any triggers? When Charissa's pastor gave a sermon on forgiveness, it triggered an extreme emotional response in her. All of a sudden she began to have difficulty breathing. After leaving the sanctuary, drinking some water, and calming herself, Charissa realized she was having a panic attack. Time was running out to forgive her aging father for his unfaithfulness to her mother. Charissa realized her desperation and set up an appointment with her pastor to help her move further on the forgiveness journey.

When we understand just how broken we are, we beg the Holy Spirit for help. Our brokenness makes us more open to the Holy Spirit. When He takes over, He gives us the courage to do what He has called us to do.

———— ⌒ ————

After you have asked yourself these questions, cry out to God, because the bottom line is this: If you want desperation for God, sometimes you have to ask Him! Take initiative and pray something like this: *Lord, I have asked myself these questions, but even these are not enough to make me desperate for You. Please, God, create in me a holy desperation for You. Show me the specific areas of my emotional script that need to be rewritten.*

REWRITING THE SCRIPT

When we recognize our need for God, become desperate for His help, and pursue Him as our only hope, *it frees us of the need to hide (shame) or to pretend to be something we aren't (pride) so that we can face our hurts in the presence of the Holy Healer.*

When I first started remembering the sexual abuse I mentioned in chapter 1, God did something very precious for me. I was in a hotel room on a prayer retreat, feeling completely overwhelmed by the enormity of the mess I was facing. I fell to my knees and began sobbing. Even though I knew in my heart that God was big enough to handle the fallout, my heart felt afraid. But instead of rehearsing old messages, I began to praise God, asking Him to replace my fear with faith.

As I did, I was transported into God's presence. Not literally, of course, but in my spirit. God gave me a vision. I saw angels surrounding God's throne and chanting in musical voices, "Holy, Holy, Holy is the Lord God Almighty." I also saw myself as a small child. Tears were streaming down my face and I was standing still, trying to disappear, so as not to be noticed. I felt frightened and didn't want anyone to know my secret. My dress was stained and torn; I felt too dirty to be in such a holy place.

In my vision, Jesus approached me gently and then said to the One on the throne, "I know this one. She is *my* child." He picked me up and clothed me in the most beautiful embroidered white dress. He washed my face and cleansed my wounds, and then He led me to the Father's lap. As I snuggled into the Abba's chest I saw a tear trickling down the Almighty's face. God the Father was crying too!

The vision ended as abruptly as it had begun, and then the Spirit of God spoke to my heart, "Becky, if you want to be healed, you must become as a little child." If I wanted a new emotional script, I had to embrace the life-giving attitude of poverty of spirit. I had to face the memories of sexual abuse in the presence of the Holy Healer so that I could replace *shame* with *loved and valued by God.*

Something to Prayerfully Consider

As we approach the end of this chapter I would like to suggest that you make a covenant with God. Would you prayerfully consider the "Covenant of the Poor in Spirit" that appears on the next page? If you are willing to make this covenant, sign your name below and date it. By signing this covenant, you are taking a step by faith toward your healing. God's presence will be continually with you as you seek His help in rewriting your script. It may seem as though you are stepping into darkness, but in reality you are taking the first step toward the sunrise.

Covenant of the Poor in Spirit

- I will embrace my brokenness and not run from it.
- I will take initiative and cry out for help from God.
- I will not build self-protective walls, but I will carefully choose a few godly people who will journey alongside me. With these few I will make every effort to be authentic and humble myself, admitting that I need prayer in the broken places of my life.

Sign and date: _____

PRAYING SCRIPTURE
TO INTERNALIZE TRUTH

Lord, I worship You because You bend down to listen (see Psalm 86:1, NKJV). You are compassionate and caring. I praise You because You are the Son of Righteousness who rises up with healing in His wings (see Malachi 4:2). I praise You, eternal God. You are my refuge and underneath me are Your everlasting arms (see Deuteronomy 33:27).

"Hear my prayer, O God; listen to the words of my mouth" (Psalm 54:2). "I am poor and needy; may the Lord think of me. You are my help and my deliverer; O my God, do not delay." Lord, answer my prayers, lift me out of the slimy pit of shame, out of the mud and mire. Set my feet on a rock and give me a firm place to stand (Psalm 40:17,2). You have called me "precious and honored" (Isaiah 43:4). Help me to internalize the truth that I am precious to You and that I don't have to live enslaved to shame. My dignity comes from You.

Lord, I am desperate for You. I am determined to seek You. "Save me, O God, for the waters have come up to my neck. I sink in the miry depths, where there is no foothold" (Psalm 69:1-2). "Answer me, O LORD, out of the goodness of your love; in your great mercy turn to me" (Psalm 69:16). Lord, I seek You. I declare with the psalmist David that those who look to You are "radiant; their faces are never covered with shame" (Psalm 34:5). Father, You have promised that You will lift up all who are bowed down (see Psalm 146:8).

My Lord, You have said that You "hate pride and arrogance" (Proverbs 8:13). You said that "pride only breeds quarrels" (Proverbs 13:10). Holy One, I bow down low before You. "O LORD God Almighty, who is like you? You are mighty, O LORD, and your faithfulness surrounds you" (Psalm 89:8). You have declared, "I am the LORD; that is my name! I will not give my glory to another" (Isaiah 42:8). Remove from me any pride or arrogance. I humble myself before You. All the praise and glory belongs to You.

I declare with the prophet Isaiah, "Surely God is my salvation; I will trust and not be afraid. The LORD, the LORD, is my strength and my song; he has become my salvation" (Isaiah 12:2). As I rewrite my emotional script I ask "that people may see and know, may consider and understand, that the hand of the LORD has done this" (Isaiah 41:20). Thank you for the indwelling Spirit of Christ, who will guide me every step of the way.

FURTHER TRANSFORMATION
Digging Deeper into the Scriptures

1. Memorize and meditate on Malachi 4:2 as written here or in another translation.

   But for you who revere my name, the sun of righteousness will rise with healing in its wings. And you will go out and leap like calves released from the stall.

2. What does it mean to you personally that the Son of righteousness will rise with healing in His wings?

3. In your own words, define what it means to become "poor in spirit." How would your life be different if you were desperate and determined for more of God?

4. Write your own definition of:
   a. Pride

b. Shame

5. Read Isaiah 14:12-15. This passage describes the fall of Satan. According to these verses, what was Satan's primary sin? Write the five "I will" statements that he made in verses 13 and 14. How do these statements reflect the sin of pride?

6. Reread the section of chapter 2 that describes shame (see pages 37-38). List reasons why a woman might feel shame.

7. What is the difference between shame and conviction?

8. Read Romans 8:1 and 1 John 1:9. Based on the truth found in these verses, what would you say to a woman who is struggling with shame because of sin she has committed?

Probing Deeper into Your Emotional Script

9. Read the story in Luke 8:40-56. Do you relate best to Jairus or to the bleeding woman? Why?

10. Read Isaiah 61:7. According to this verse, what is the promise for the person who has struggled with shame but chooses to bring his or her shame to God? Write a paraphrase of this verse in your own words. What does this promise mean to you personally?

11. Review the section of chapter 2 titled "Getting in Touch with Desperation" (pages 38-41). Sit quietly before God. Ask the Holy Spirit to search your heart. Then journal your answers to each of the four questions in that section:

a. Do I have any patterns of behavior that I am trying to keep secret?

b. Do I have any broken or strained relationships?

c. Have I believed any lies that are holding me back from all that God has for me? What lies are written in my emotional script?

d. Do any of my emotional responses feel like an overreaction? Are these related to coping mechanisms? Can I identify any triggers?

12. Unleash the power of praise. Take a worship walk. Listen to praise music. Allow the music to prompt your praise. Praise God that He has released you by faith from shame.

CHAPTER 3

GRIEVE YOUR LOSSES

Blessed are those who mourn.

MATTHEW 5:4

K risten asked me, "I just want a father. Why couldn't my dad be different? Why didn't God allow me to have the kind of father my friends have?" When she was only four years old Kristen's dad decided that the responsibilities of being a husband and father were too much and he walked out the door. As a result of this confusing and painful experience, *rejection* and *abandonment* were written on Kristen's emotional script. Convinced her father's abandonment was her fault, Kristen grew up believing he would be the father she longed for, if only she could figure out how to please him.

At various times during her growing-up years, Kristen's father would reenter her life. Every time, her hopes would rise and she would try to perform better, believing somewhere deep down inside, "Surely I can do something differently to make him love me." She bought him gifts and wrote him cards, always thinking these would encourage him to stay in her life. Always, her efforts ended in disappointment.

Kristen had come to me after receiving yet another letter from her father, rejecting all her efforts at salvaging their relationship. The realization finally hit her: Her biological father was not able or willing to be the father she wanted. She was going to have to lay down all expectations that he would change. But laying down expectations would happen only amid a lot of tears.

The weeping that Kristen did that night was only the beginning of her grieving process. She needed to give voice to all the sorrow she felt, to mourn all of her losses. She had to grieve all the fun activities that most little girls enjoy but that she had missed with her daddy. She needed to mourn the nights she wished he had tucked her into bed and given her butterfly kisses. She needed to grieve the devastation she felt when he didn't show up to her ballet recitals or school plays. She had to mourn every forgotten birthday. Each loss brought a fresh flood of tears.

To move forward and bring closure to the father wounds of her childhood, Kristen had to allow all those buried wounds to bubble to the surface. As long as she tried to keep them at bay, she could not make progress in rewriting her script. She had to weep in order to cleanse the toxic wounds of her father's abandonment. As she took her grief to God, He began to heal her and change her from the inside out.

We too need to get in touch with our pain and grieve our hurts and disappointments if we want to change and rewrite our emotional scripts. I believe that is why Jesus said, "Blessed are those who mourn" (Matthew 5:4). We generally think of mourning only for someone who dies. But I think Jesus had a whole lot more in mind.

How Grieving Helps Us

The only path of healing is through the valley of mourning. That's where the rub often comes, because we don't like to feel pain or sorrow. We run from it, hide from it, anesthetize it. We do anything to not feel it. And we certainly don't want to express it. As a result, we want to "get over" whatever has caused the hurt, which tempts us to skip the mourning. But if we do this, we won't completely heal. Steve Arterburn has written, "When we resist grieving, we drag our pain with us all through our lives."[1]

I wanted to know why grieving and mourning are so crucial to rewriting our emotional script, so I asked several friends who are professional counselors to help me understand why this beatitude is so important. Here are some of their insights:

- Grieving the harmful and destructive messages written on our emotional scripts when we were children opens our hearts and souls so that the Lord can heal and cleanse us. It helps provide the closure we need. If the grieving doesn't happen, we are left with all those feelings stuck inside of us, and we can wallow endlessly with those emotions. —Kris

- When we avoid grieving the losses and hurts we experienced in childhood, the negative messages they imprinted on our scripts continue to cause problems in our lives . . . emotionally, spiritually, and physically. Emotionally we get stuck (depressed, angry), spiritually we get angry at God (question Him, turn from Him), and physically we can become ill. To enter into the grieving process is to experience growth and life-transforming change through Jesus Christ. —Dena

- Mourning the losses we experienced in childhood is important because of what it produces in us. As we go through the process of mourning, we grieve our losses and draw near to God. He is able to heal our wounds in a way that creates softness in our hearts, making us ready for change in a righteous direction. Once we have gone through this process, we know that God will always grow and transform us through our trials and sufferings. This blesses us. —Susan

Let me summarize their comments: Mourning brings closure to the hurts written on our emotional scripts and tenderizes our hearts for new scripts. If we don't grieve our losses, we stuff them, and our emotional scripts don't get rewritten. As a result, we continue using the same old coping mechanisms. This can cause us to make choices that are even more unhealthful than those we've made before.

When Jesus said, "Blessed are those who mourn," He knew what He was talking about. The word He used for mourning carries the idea of lamentation or extreme sorrow.[2]

TO MOURN OR LAMENT MEANS:

I give voice to the anguish of my soul.

In case you are thinking, Doesn't Scripture tell us to rejoice in all things?[3] If so, doesn't this mean we should just suck it up and rejoice, no matter what happens? Let me assure you that Scripture tells the stories of several biblical characters who openly expressed great pain and sorrow over things that God allowed to happen to them and those they loved. All of these men were deeply spiritual, and yet they brought their grief into their relationships with God. Let's look at how they did this, because if we want to rewrite our emotional scripts, we must do the same with our past hurts.

BIBLICAL EXAMPLES OF LAMENTING

Remember Job? Satan went before God, asking permission to test His servant Job. Satan's theory was that Job worshipped God only because the Almighty had blessed him. So, with God's permission, Satan tore apart Job's world. His children died; he lost all his sheep and camels; his entire livelihood was stripped away. To make matters worse, Job's friends attacked and criticized him, saying he must have sinned terribly and that he had no right to question God.

Job's story makes you think twice about whom you want as your friends in times of deep suffering, doesn't it? Your real friends will crawl into the suffering with you. They will not judge or give advice on how to "get over it." They won't try to "fix you" and talk you out of what you're feeling. Instead, they will weep with you, understanding that sorrow doesn't always make sense and that sometimes all you can do is weep.

It is in this context that Job said, "Therefore I will not keep silent; I will speak out in the anguish of my spirit, I will complain in the bitterness of my soul" (Job 7:11). Wow! I love that Job had the courage to face his well-meaning, spiritual-sounding friends and say, "You know what, guys? I am not going to listen to you! Instead, I *will* express my anguish to the Lord. I *will* cry out in the bitterness of my raw pain." Job didn't try to clean up his feelings or make them more presentable. His feelings were raw, and he expressed them openly and honestly. He held nothing back.

Job isn't the only biblical character who expressed deep pain through mourning. So did Jeremiah. He was a prophet who watched his friends become captives. Jerusalem had been captured by the Babylonians. The temple and the throne were both gone, and their destruction seemed to be the end of King David's dynasty. From a human perspective it appeared as though God had gone back on His promise that David's kingdom would have no end (see 2 Samuel 7:16). Jeremiah felt that God had abandoned him. He wrote:

> He has driven me away and made me walk in darkness rather than light; indeed, he has turned his hand against me again and again, all day long. . . . He has walled me in so I cannot escape; he has weighed me down with chains. Even when I call out or cry for help, he shuts out my prayer. He has barred my way with blocks of stone; he has made my paths crooked. (Lamentations 3:2-3,7-9)

As he processed his feelings authentically, Jeremiah finally came to the point of remembering the Lord's faithfulness. After he had emptied himself of all his grief, he was finally able to see the truth that those losses had been blocking: God is indeed good.

I can relate to Jeremiah. He gives words to some of the pain I have longed to express to God but could not articulate on my own. Because of the wounds in my emotional script as well as my genetic makeup, I too have struggled with depression from time to time. Some of my depression was deep sadness. Some of it was unresolved anger turned inward. Some of it was complete emotional exhaustion due to cancer, six surgeries, sexual abuse memories, moves to different areas of the country, and a host of other stresses over the course of a five-year period.

Part of the answer to my depression lay in medication. Many Christians hesitate to take an antidepressant, fearing that this is unspiritual. To me this seems unwise because the brain is an organ, part of our physical body. At times it becomes exhausted and needs help. Rather than battle lack of energy and low motivation, I prefer to take an antidepressant and have the energy to be who God has called me to be. If you are unsure about whether you need an antidepressant, ask your health care provider for an evaluation. Antidepressants can help some people.

Another part of the answer was learning to lament the wounds of my childhood. I grew up with a script that read that anger was wrong, so for years I stuffed my anger at those who had hurt me. I was even angry at God. In order to change my script I had to question God, honestly asking, "Where were You during the abuse? I felt abandoned by You." Rather than denying or stuffing my anger, I had to learn to let it out in healthy ways. Instead of turning my anger inward, I expressed it in my journal, in my prayers to God, and with a few close spiritually mature friends.

I grew to understand that anger can be productive. It can motivate me to ask, "What can I do to change this situation?" It can encourage me to speak out for justice, and it can empower me to set boundaries. I began to think of anger as a red flag signaling that something needs to be resolved. The more I paid attention to those red flags and released my anger in healthy ways, the less depressed I felt.

King David is another biblical character who can show us something about how to lament our hurts. He cried out, "How long, O LORD? Will you forget me forever? . . . How long must I wrestle with my thoughts and every day have sorrow in my heart?" (Psalm 13:1-2). David also begged God to break the teeth of his enemies (see Psalm 3:7). Now there's a prayer you can get your hands around! And you thought it was wrong to get angry? You thought God couldn't handle your rage? Maybe you, like me, need to rewrite the messages in your script about anger so that you can begin to express it honestly to God.

Even Jesus, the perfect Son of God, gave voice to the anguish in His soul. Here are several scenes from the Gospels where the Son of God lamented. Join me as we take a look at each:

Scene One: Jesus is riding on the back of a colt. The air is filled with exuberant excitement. As He comes near the place where the road goes down the Mount of Olives, the crowd begins cheering and shouting. Praises fill the air. In loud voices the onlookers joyfully chant, "Blessed is the king who comes in the name of the Lord!" (Luke 19:38). As Jesus approaches Jerusalem, the mood changes. The Son of God begins to weep. He laments with cries of "if only." He laments, "Oh Jerusalem, if only you had known this day was coming. If only you had repented. If only you had listened" (Luke 19:42, author's paraphrase). The stubborn sinfulness of Jerusalem breaks the heart of God.

Scene Two: In this scene darkness shrouds the garden where Jesus is kneeling before the Father, weeping. It is hours before His death. He knows what is coming and He pleads with Father God, "If you are willing, take this cup from me" (Luke 22:42). In other words, Jesus moans, "Oh God, I don't want to do this." As He pours out His tortured soul, questioning the Father and begging for another way, His anguish is so great that He "sweat . . . drops of blood" (verse 44). Luke is speaking metaphorically here. Christ did not actually sweat blood. What Luke wants us to understand is the depth of the emotional agony that Christ felt. His pain was so intense that it caused His perspiration to fall like clotted blood.

Scene Three: While Jesus is hanging on the cross, He questions, "My God, my God, why have you forsaken me?" (Mark 15:34). It is His darkest, most desperate hour. He is undergoing unimaginable suffering, both spiritually and physically. His soul and spirit are covered with the slime and shame of your sin and mine. His body is bruised, broken, and bloody. God the Father's presence is nowhere to be found. The Father, the perfect Father, has abandoned His Son during His darkest hour.

This is mind-boggling. What kind of father abandons his son? What kind of father refuses to step in to defend his innocent kid? What kind of father walks away from his battered and bruised child? Sinful fathers at times forsake their kids. Sinful fathers at times abuse and abandon their children. But can't we expect more from the perfect, Holy Father, who claims to be love? I have wrestled with these questions, and I don't know the answer. It is paradoxical. The Cross seems both God the Father's cruelest moment and, at the same time, His greatest demonstration of grace. Still, I find great comfort in this scene. It shows me that Jesus has experienced the pain of feeling abandoned. Those of us, like Kristen, who have felt abandoned by our earthly fathers can follow His example and cry out in utter desperation, "Why?"

Of course, all of these biblical examples are about people who were grieving current suffering and pain, which we must do as well. But if we want to rewrite our emotional scripts, it is not enough to simply grieve the losses we've faced as adults; we must also grieve our childhood losses, because these are the hurts that likely have done the most damage to our emotional scripts. What do these biblical examples show us about how we must grieve our past hurts in order to rewrite our emotional scripts?

GRIEVING THE PAIN OF YOUR PAST

As I have considered this question, I have come up with four practical steps that help me voice my anguish. My prayer is that they will help you as well.

Step 1: Embrace the Darkness

Facing our pasts is like walking into a dark, scary closet. You never know what skeletons might jump out at you. If you face them, you might have to face pain. So you stand outside the door, debating. The problem is, if you stand outside too long, it's easy to imagine that the skeletons in the closet are worse than they really are. On the other hand, you might pretend that everything in that closet is just fine; no skeletons in *your* closet. That's called denial. Ah . . . denial. It may seem like a good plan at first and very tempting, but denial *never* helps us find healing and freedom. Instead, it locks the door behind us, and then we find ourselves stuck in the very closet we wanted to avoid.

If you take a flashlight, dark closets are far less scary. So tell the Lord you're ready. Invite Him into your past. He calls Himself the Light of the World (see John 8:12). He's more than willing to illumine what you need to know. He said, "Then you will know the truth, and the truth will set you free" (John 8:32). Then, with the presence of Christ, face any dark memories He directs you to and embrace your brokenness.

So how do we walk into the closets of our pasts? How do we embrace the darkness? One practical way is by keeping a journal. Write down your reflections on your childhood. Record your feelings and patterns of feelings. Be gut-level honest. Sometimes finding my feelings is hard. I often write prayers to the Lord that go like this: *Dear Lord, I think what I am feeling today is sadness. Holy One, it feels as though my heart is ripping. I feel as if I don't have enough energy to face the day.* When you don't understand your feelings, write a prayer to God, asking Him to give you insight and wisdom: *Father, I don't understand why I am feeling this way today. Help me to see what's behind the sadness.* Keeping a journal helps us face our feelings.

If we want to rewrite our emotional scripts, we must not run from the painful things in our pasts, no matter how great the loss or how big the mess. Instead, we must choose to face those hurts and learn to grieve. Only then can those losses "function as a catalyst to transform us."[4]

Step 2: List the Hurts That Warped Your Script

Until you identify all that has twisted your emotional script, you cannot mourn those losses. For example, when our family left a church where we had experienced great hurt, a wise friend and mentor encouraged my husband to make a list of everything he had lost. Steve felt skeptical. Why focus on the negative when he was trying to move beyond the hurt? Yet, because his friend was so persistent, Steve went ahead and made his list. He had lost his career, financial security, reputation, status in the eyes of other pastors, and his identity as a pastor, to name just a few. On and on his list went. As Steve considered this list, tears welled up in his eyes. My husband does not cry easily. But the Holy Spirit knew Steve needed to grieve if he was to get closure.

Susan also made a list of her past hurts and losses. She had grown up in a boarding school where she was hurt by too many spankings from overly strict teachers and by her parents' physical and emotional separation. (She saw them only once a year because they were missionaries on a faraway island.) As she wrote her list of losses, she allowed the tears to flow. While Susan respected her parents' ministry, she realized she needed to grieve the losses she suffered as a result of growing up in a boarding school. Once she listed those losses, she was able to lament each of them.

Step 3: Get in Touch with the Pain

Tears are the cleansing mechanism that God uses to wash the wounds of our souls. Never underestimate the power of a good cry! As author Michael Card has written, "Weeping has an honored place in the life of faith."[5] Wounds that aren't washed become infected. Great works of healing are performed in the flood of torrential tears. King David understood how important tears were. He wrote, "You have collected all my tears in your bottle" (Psalm 56:8, NLT). Imagine—God considers your tears so precious that He collects them and treasures them. David was well-acquainted with weeping. We are told that at one point in his life he wept until he had no more strength left (see 1 Samuel 30:4).

When I need to cry I turn on worship music. Music helps me get in touch with pain. Praise music softens my heart and also reminds me that God loves me. During the years when I was facing the abuse memories, I turned on worship music early in the morning. I got on my knees and knelt in front of my couch. Listening to the worship music tenderized my heart. Often, I buried my face in the cushion and wept. I worshipped God with my tears. That couch became known as my "weeping couch," and after a while there was a huge stain on the light blue cushion. But I didn't care, because I knew the mark represented the tears God was collecting as I bowed every memory before Him. Personally, I think we all need a weeping couch. All of us have painful messages that need to be erased. What better place to weep than before the Lord?

Tears might come for you during a church service. Don't be embarrassed. When we worship, the Holy Spirit unlocks the doors of truth in our lives. Sometimes that means you are going to cry, even during corporate worship. That's okay. Don't suppress your tears; they are God's instruments of healing and cleansing.

Step 4: Question God

Yes, you read that right. Question. Wrestle. Complain to God. Tell Him you felt abandoned as a child. Ask Him where He was. God is big enough to handle your questions. Remember, even Jesus questioned God. As you wrestle with and complain to God, you are emptying your heart of its hurts. Teach yourself to pour out your heart to God.

Ask God why and where? *Why did You allow this, God? And where are You?* That's what Martha did. Because she had polio when she was a little girl, she spent a lot of time in and out of hospitals. The disease left her crippled and unable to play the games most children play. Many times while sitting on the sidelines while other children played dodgeball or jump rope, Martha felt lonely. Years later, when Martha analyzed how polio affected her emotional script, she began to question God, "Why did You let that happen to me?" What a great question! Sometimes God may give you the answer, sometimes He may not.

Many women who are survivors of sexual abuse have asked God these questions, including me. Whenever I have questioned God, He has never punished me for doing so. Instead, I have felt strangely closer to Him after venting my feelings to Him. In the dark night of the soul's deepest sorrow, we need to give voice to the honest, scary questions of our hearts. Giving voice to those questions releases the poison inside.

A PLAN FOR HOW TO COPE

When I was mourning the losses of my childhood, feeling the pain from my past, the hurt threatened to overwhelm me, so I came up with the following plan. It helped me function even though the pain from my past felt so great. I pray that it helps you too.

1. Get out of bed and make the bed so I don't get back in it!
2. Take a worship walk. Exercise releases endorphins. Praise releases the Holy Spirit. On these walks, I praise God for who He is and not for my circumstances.
3. Focus on one passage of Scripture. It might be only one verse. But filling my mind with Scripture protects it from the discouraging messages Satan wants me to dwell on.
4. Accomplish two tasks. These might be as simple as loading the dishwasher or folding laundry.
5. Encourage one person. One dark day I went to the grocery store (one of my tasks) and on a whim I paid for an elderly woman's groceries. It encouraged her heart and lifted mine!

Sometimes I might call a friend or send a package to my
child away at college.

6. Rest, weep, and regroup. While I've included weeping
   here, the truth is that weeping can't be scheduled. Feelings
   of grief come and go throughout the day. But after I have
   accomplished two tasks I give myself permission to rest: I lie
   down, read a relaxing book, bake, or do something else that
   relaxes me.

7. Reflect on the day and record three good things that
   happened that day.

This plan has been a lifesaver for me, whether I'm grieving past or
present hurts. It's only seven things. It doesn't feel overwhelming. By
the end of the day, usually the darkness has lifted. It doesn't take away
my valley of weeping, as David called it (see Psalm 84, NLT). Instead, it
gives me the courage to continue on through the valley of weeping.

The valley of weeping often feels never-ending. We wonder, *Will I
ever stop hurting completely?* I have been asked this question, and honestly, I don't know. I know that I still hurt, but I also know it hurts less.
Kristen, whom you met at the beginning of this chapter, would say
that God has healed her. She is erasing the lies on her emotional script
and replacing them with God's healing attitudes and truth. Yet every
now and then something will trigger the old feelings of abandonment,
and she will cry all over again. That's because grief comes in waves. We
may grieve for a while and think we are done grieving a particular hurt
or loss, only to find ourselves crying all over again at some later date.
That's okay. Even when there has been healing, it doesn't necessarily
take away the sadness. But that doesn't mean we are without comfort.

FINDING COMFORT

I wonder: *When God the Father looks back at Calvary, does He
feel the pain all over again of having to abandon His Son?* He knows
immeasurable good has come out of the Crucifixion. He knows the

Resurrection happened. But I still wonder, if in looking back at the Cross, God the Father doesn't shed a tear about the horror of it all. When we think back on the horror we have experienced, even when we know God has used it for good, many of us will shed a tear as well. Thankfully, God offers comfort in the midst of our lamenting. Without His promise of comfort, the temptation to quit would feel intense.

Where is this comfort that is promised? How do we experience it when we are grieving the losses of past pain? As I have questioned God on this issue, He has shown me several ways we experience His comfort.

Through Community

Remember, we cannot rewrite our emotional scripts alone. We need others in the body of Christ to walk alongside, cheer us on, and comfort us when the journey feels long and hard. God designed us for community, so it makes sense that one of the sources of comfort on our journey of rewriting the script will be others who come alongside.

Comfort through the body of Christ is available to all of us. The problem for many of us comes when we hide our hurts in an effort to look as though we have it all together. As a result, we fail to cry for help. I wonder how much comfort we miss out on because we are too proud to admit we are broken and hurting. Ask God to bring someone into your life with whom you can be honest. Then take a risk and choose to trust that person by telling her about the hurts in your past.

Through Camaraderie with Biblical Heroes

Throughout this chapter we have looked at several biblical heroes who expressed their anguish to God in the midst of very painful circumstances. When I need comfort, I often reread the story of Joseph (see Genesis 37–50), who was sold into slavery at a young age by his jealous brothers. His story reminds me that God can take the messiest childhood and use it in amazing ways. (We will take a closer look at Joseph in chapter 8.) God has given us these stories through His Word so that we will find comfort and understanding from those who have gone before us.

Here are some of the biblical characters who give me hope. I pray their examples give you hope as well.

- David — Psalm 5; 42:5,11
- Mary and Martha — John 11
- Naomi — Ruth 1:20
- Hannah — 1 Samuel 1:10
- Mary Magdalene — John 20:10-16

Through the Continual Presence of the Holy Spirit

The Holy Spirit is called the Comforter. Jesus told His grieving disciples that it was for their good that He go away, because if He left, the Counselor, the Comforter, would come to them. He would be with them, and He would also be in them (see John 16:7).

How does the Holy Spirit comfort us? He may bring a Scripture verse to memory, reminding us of His love in a dark moment when we feel unloved. He may bring the words of a praise song to our hearts when we toss and turn in the night because life feels so hard. He may allow us to feel a deeper sense of His presence when we feel lost and alone.

If you and I are going to rewrite our emotional scripts, we must give voice to the anguish in our hearts about the things that have wounded us. It is my conviction that only after we weep, only after we question, can we bow to God's sovereignty. In the clashing of our wills, in the chaos of confusion, we collapse exhausted against the chest of almighty God. There He comforts and holds us as we acknowledge that He is God and we are not.

Before we move on to the next chapter, where we will look at surrendering control, I would like to encourage you to buy a journal if you haven't already. Get alone with God. Spend at least an hour with Him.

Write down reflections of your childhood. List your losses. Ask God if there's any weeping you need to do. It's possible you may have already shed lots of tears over your childhood. If you have, write a prayer in your journal, thanking God for the tears, and then spend some time reflecting on how those tears have helped you.

PRAYING SCRIPTURE
TO INTERNALIZE TRUTH

Lord Jesus, I worship You as the Man of Sorrows who was very familiar with suffering (see Isaiah 53:3). I praise You because You take up my infirmities and carry my sorrows (see Isaiah 53:4). Thank you, Holy One, for inviting me to lament.

"Hear my prayer, O LORD; let my cry for help come to you. Do not hide your face from me when I am in distress." Holy One, I need You. "Turn your ear to me; when I call, answer me" (Psalm 102:1-2). Lord, "my tears have been my food day and night" (Psalm 42:3). I feel as though I am drowning in sorrow. "Save me, O God, for the waters have come up to my neck. . . . I am worn out calling for help; my throat is parched. My eyes fail, looking for my God" (Psalm 69:1,3). Lord, "I cry out to you . . . but you do not answer" (Job 30:20). You are called Immanuel, meaning God with us (see Isaiah 7:14). I cannot feel Your presence. Where are You, Lord? I cry out with the psalmist, "My soul is in anguish. How long, O LORD, how long? . . . I am worn out from groaning; all night long I flood my bed with weeping and drench my couch with tears" (Psalm 6:3,6).

Lord, Your Word tells me that Your love reaches to the heavens and Your faithfulness to the skies (see Psalm 36:5). Why then did You allow this great sorrow in my life? "Why must I go about mourning?" (Psalm 43:2). When will the waves of grief stop flooding over me? "O LORD, you have seen this; be not silent. Do not be far from me" (Psalm 35:22). Lord, my worship is my weeping. "Yet this I call to mind and therefore I have hope: Because of the LORD's great love [I am] not consumed, for his compassions never fail. They are new every morning; great is your faithfulness" (Lamentations 3:21-23).

Holy One, though You bring grief will You not show compassion? (see Lamentations 3:32). Yet, my hope is in You. I know I will praise You again. "Weeping may remain for a night, but rejoicing comes in the morning" (Psalm 30:5). "Send forth your light and your truth, let them guide me; let them bring me to your holy mountain, to the place where you dwell" (Psalm 43:3).

God, I don't profess to understand Your ways. Who has known the mind of the Lord? Or who has been His counselor? Who has given to God, that God should repay him? For from Him and through Him and to Him are all things. To You alone, O Lord, be the glory (see Romans 11:34-36). "The Lord gave and the Lord has taken away; may the name of the Lord be praised" (Job 1:21). Though I do not understand Your ways, O Lord, I choose to fall down and worship You.

FURTHER TRANSFORMATION
Digging Deeper into the Scriptures

1. Meditate on and memorize Lamentations 3:22-25, as written here or in another Bible version.

   Because of the LORD's great love we are not consumed,
   for his compassions never fail.
   They are new every morning;
   great is your faithfulness.

2. Write a definition of lamenting using your own words.

3. Read Psalm 42. What emotions did David express in this psalm? List the ways he lamented. What questions did he ask God? How did he find comfort?

4. Read Isaiah 61:1-3. Isaiah wrote these words describing the ministry of Jesus. What promises can you find in these verses for those who are mourning?

5. Read John 16:7. The Holy Spirit is called the Comforter. Jesus
   told His disciples that it was better that He go away. Why? How
   have you personally experienced the comfort of the Holy Spirit?

Probing Deeper into Your Emotional Script

6. As you read on page 60, Michael Card wrote, "Weeping has an
   honored place in the life of faith." Do you agree or disagree with
   this statement? Why? Do you feel embarrassed when you cry?
   Why or why not?

7. The Psalms are like an open journal of David's emotions. Why do
   you think God included the Psalms in the Bible? Do you keep a
   journal? Why or why not? How could a journal help you express
   your emotions more honestly to God?

8. Read Luke 22:39-46. Describe the emotions in this scene. What was Christ feeling? Would you say He was depressed? Why or why not? Describe a time when you felt depressed.

9. How have you personally experienced tangible comfort through community? How might you bring comfort to someone who is rewriting a painful emotional script? List your ideas below.

10. What have you learned from this chapter about the importance of mourning? If you were to explain to a friend why mourning or lamenting is so important, what would you say?

11. Write your own prayer of lament to God. Express your sorrow over a painful part of your childhood.

12. Unleash the power of praise. Write every letter of the alphabet here. Next to each letter, write down one (or more) attribute of God that begins with that letter. Then read back over your list slowly. Praise God for each of those attributes.
    For example:
    a. Lord, You are Almighty.
    b. God, You are Beautiful.

CHAPTER 4

LET GO OF
CONTROL

Blessed are the meek.

MATTHEW 5:5

I lay in bed unable to sleep, my mind active with worry. Earlier that day my daughter had called to say her car had caught on fire. Smoke was billowing out of the engine and she had to pull over on the side of the road and walk to a house for help. She was thousands of miles away at college, and I felt so out of control! By this time of night the problem had been solved and my daughter was safely back in her dorm room, but my mind was spinning off frantic scenarios of what could have happened. Finally, I prayed, *Lord, help! I have a problem. I want to trust You, but I can't seem to do that. I say I trust You with my mouth, but I don't feel trust in my heart. You know me better than anyone else. Will You help me change my emotional script so that I can trust You?*

God was more than willing.

He longed to have me trust Him, and so He used a counselor to show me areas of my life that had been violated by a man whom I had trusted as a little girl. The person who had sexually abused me had damaged my ability to trust and my concept of God. He had robbed me of innocence and stolen my sense of safety. I felt powerless against him. He professed to love God and even served Him; consequently, deep inside I feared that God was on the side of my abuser, who often said to me, "Becky, nothing can happen to you out of the sovereign will of God." As a result of those words, I developed a faulty view of God, one that said He couldn't be trusted.

As a result of this message, fear reigned supreme in my life and played out in many ways. I worried a lot. I obsessed about the safety of my children. I second-guessed myself a lot. Had I made the right decision? Had I heard God correctly? Fear tormented my thoughts with questions: *How do you know God will protect you? How do you know He will protect your children? Maybe He's punishing you.*

When fear sits in the driver's seat, control issues are sure to follow. The desire to control our lives is birthed out of fear, fear that something bad is going to happen to us or those we care about. Those of us who grew up in situations that felt chaotic and out of control have emotional scripts that have been twisted by the fear that something bad could happen to us at any moment. Fear leads our minds down the roads of "what if" and "what then" scenarios.

Consequently, we begin to rely on our own abilities to reestablish order in our chaotic worlds. We try to build security and structure with our own hands rather than relying on God to provide these things for us. As a result, disruptive patterns of control show up in the most unexpected ways and at the most inopportune times. What are some of these patterns?

- Worry or anxiety
- Manipulation
- Nagging
- Eating issues
- Bossiness

- Rigidity
- Black-and-white thinking (an all-or-nothing attitude)
- Difficulty delegating
- Workaholic patterns
- Tension
- Perfectionism

Here are a few examples of how these patterns play out:

- As soon as we are handed that birth certificate, we're convinced that our children are deserving of any and every honor. We want to be sure our babies are not overlooked. So what do we do? We try to control their destinies.
- We become frustrated with the progress of God's working in our lives or in the lives of those close to us, and we decide to "help out."
- We feel powerless over some areas of our lives, and so we overcompensate and "take charge" in other ways.
- We feel we cannot trust others to do a job, so we perform the task ourselves. As a result, we become frazzled and stressed from taking on responsibility that was never intended to be ours in the first place.

Have you seen any of these symptoms in your mirror lately? If so, you likely have fear written on your emotional script. Left unchecked, fear eventually leads us to believe the lie that says, "The only way I can feel safe is if I am in control." That's when we know we are in trouble, because God's Word teaches that we're not the ones to be in control. God is. He is called "the blessed controller of all things" (1 Timothy 6:15, PH). He is not a "bad" controller but a "blessed" controller. The problem with taking control is that control is built on self-reliance and bypasses the need for God-reliance.

Jesus' prescription for purging our emotional scripts of fear and control is found in the next beatitude: "Blessed are the meek, for they will inherit the earth" (Matthew 5:5).

The Antidote to Fear and Control

Praus, the Greek word translated in this beatitude as *meek,* "denotes gentle, mild, or meek."[1] Throughout Scripture *meekness* isn't used to refer to a person's natural disposition. Instead, it refers to an "inwrought grace of the soul."[2] It speaks of "humility and trust in God."[3]

TO PUT ON MEEKNESS MEANS:

*I surrender all of myself to God
and submit to His plans for my life.*

All of us are self-absorbed. We think about ourselves, worry about ourselves, defend ourselves, and promote ourselves. However, when we choose meekness, we become Christ-absorbed. As a result of our surrender, the Holy Spirit develops in us a gentle and gracious attitude.

Meekness is not a natural personality trait. It is a Spirit-developed attitude. This is important for us to understand, because otherwise some of us could excuse ourselves from meekness by rationalizing that we just have strong personalities. Each of us is born with a personality and temperament. (Again, this is our emotional script, the lens through which we view life.) Some are quiet and gentle by nature. Others are loud and strong-willed by nature. Some are easygoing. Others could be described as high-strung. But no matter our temperaments, Jesus calls us to surrender all of self to Him and to put on meekness.

Meekness is the polar opposite of control.

---

*Control = Self-Reliance
Meekness = God-Reliance*

Jesus said, "Come to me, all you who are weary and burdened, and I will give you rest. Take my yoke upon you and learn from me, for I am gentle and humble in heart, and you will find rest for your souls. For my yoke is easy and my burden is light" (Matthew 11:28-30). When we stop trying to control our lives and instead give our concerns over to God, we are choosing meekness. Most of the issues we feel fearful and anxious about are things or circumstances we cannot control. Think about it: What are the issues you are most concerned with right now? What are your burdens? How many of those can you control? Jesus said His yoke is easy and His burden is light. If yours feels heavy, is it possible that you are having difficulty surrendering control? The rest Jesus spoke of here is release from the heaviness of those burdens. When we take control, we carry the burden ourselves. When we surrender, God carries the burden. As A. W. Tozer wrote, "We cease to do."[4] We let go of the things we cannot control. As a result we can rest.

It's particularly difficult to surrender control when we are undergoing threatening or heartbreaking circumstances. When bad things happen, we begin to question and doubt God's goodness. We wonder, "Does He really know what's best for my life?" Our old script tells us to not surrender because, after all, who wants to trust a God who slam-dunks us? That's one reason why we must grieve our losses as often as necessary. Even if we have grieved and yielded to God's sovereignty, we sometimes have to continue grieving and yielding. But if we humble ourselves and yield, we learn that God is more than able to carry our burdens. When we release our concerns to Him, we find that we naturally become more peaceful, less tense, less stressed-out and anxious. The Spirit weaves a new softness into our souls. I have seen this in my friend and mentor, Linda Dillow.

Years ago when her children were teens, Linda made some powerful choices to rewrite her emotional script and surrender all control to God. The rewriting she did years ago has paid off. Recently, Linda's world spun out of control when she passed out in an airport, fell down sixteen steps, and suffered a serious blow to her skull. As a result of the severe concussion that she experienced, Linda has had to surrender control in many areas of her life, including her schedule and her health. The pace of her life has had to change. Her low energy level has forced her to slow down significantly, even to the point of canceling many speaking engagements. The adjustment has been difficult, yet I have watched my precious friend handle these new physical challenges with gentleness and graciousness. The softness the Holy Spirit has woven into Linda's soul has been a powerful example for me.

Before we talk about what meekness looks like, I'd like to clear up some of the common misconceptions about it in case you need to correct your understanding of this beatitude.

CLEARING UP COMMON MISCONCEPTIONS

Does rewriting your script and surrendering control require you to kiss your rights good-bye and become a doormat? Definitely not, and those who think so don't understand what meekness is.

Misconception #1: Meekness Slams Our Self-Esteem

Meekness is *not* low self-esteem; it does not mean thinking poorly of ourselves. On the contrary, the meek person possesses a better understanding of who she is in Christ, and as a result she has nothing to prove. She doesn't need to control everything in order to feel worthwhile. She possesses a quiet inner confidence that allows her to rest assured. She knows God is in control. She knows she doesn't need to take charge to be valuable. She is free to lead, but realizes that God is the one in charge.

WHO YOU ARE IN CHRIST

Holy and dearly loved—Colossians 3:12

Adopted as His children—Galatians 4:5-7; Ephesians 1:4-5

Heirs with Christ—Romans 8:16-18

Precious and honored—Isaiah 43:4

Friends of God—John 15:14-15

A Royal Priest—1 Peter 2:9

The Bride of Christ—Revelation 19:7-8

Misconception #2: Meekness Blurs Our Boundaries

Perhaps you're thinking, *What about the woman who is in an abusive relationship? Is she supposed to surrender all her rights to an abusive husband?* No! Meekness never calls us to surrender to a person who is abusing or hurting us. It calls us to surrender to a perfect, loving God.

The woman who is a doormat or stays in an abusive relationship has a problem with boundaries. Boundaries are the limits we set for ourselves. They are invisible lines that protect us from becoming enmeshed with other people or being taken advantage of by them. One woman has said that boundaries are like property lines. I have to learn I am responsible for only my property. That means I'm not going to step outside of my boundaries and try to fix you, because you are not my property.

It also means that I am not going to allow you to step inside my boundaries, because I am not your property. Boundaries empower us to say no. They protect us from burnout and resentment. When our boundaries become blurred, we lose ourselves in other people's demands and our priorities become lost. If we live without boundaries, we can become what and who others want us to be, but we fail to be who God has uniquely designed us to be.

For example, if you say yes every time someone at your church asks you to take on some new ministry because you can't say no, you will eventually become burned out. Chances are you will not be doing the very thing God has called you to do. God never calls us to burn out. However, if you take on meekness, it will enable you to say yes only to the things to which God has called you—and to say no to everything else. God has uniquely gifted you and given you specific talents. He needs only one you, and *you* are too precious to self-destruct.

Meekness doesn't cloud our boundaries—it actually clarifies them, because it helps us understand what we can control and what we cannot. This has certainly been the case for me. I once received a phone call from a woman who lived hundreds of miles away who was threatening to commit suicide. She was not emotionally well and wanted me to drop everything and drive hundreds of miles to be by her side. I could not do that because I had commitments with my kids and husband. As I lay in bed that night thinking and worrying, I realized that it was okay for me to tell her I couldn't come. The Holy Spirit reminded me that I could not control her choice, and that thinking I could solve her problem would have meant I had an inflated ego. The only thing I could do was pray for her, and that I did. But prayer was my limit.

When we put on meekness, we realize our limits. When we put on meekness, we realize we can't be all things to all people. That is God's job. Meekness helps us to trust God with His job—taking care of all people. When we trust Him with His job, we know where to set our boundaries.

Even though I have been rewriting my script and doing my best to erase messages of fear that prompt me to take control, sometimes appropriate boundaries can still be blurry for me. In those moments I have learned to pray, *Lord, I want to put on meekness. I want to give up who I am and embrace all of who You are. But, Lord, help me to lose myself only in You and not in other people. Show me how to put on meekness by setting clear boundaries.*

Misconception #3: Meekness Equals Weakness

As you'll see in the next section, meekness doesn't mean weakness. Meekness is the strength of character, even in times of great pressure, to surrender control of our lives to God and cooperate with His plans for our lives. We see this strength of character in Moses, who was called the meekest of all men (Numbers 12:3, KJV). The Jewish people had been in bondage in Egypt for years, and the Israelites were crying out to God for help. God heard their groaning and raised up Moses to lead them out of bondage.

When God first asked Moses to lead His people out of slavery, Moses felt so insecure that he literally begged God to send someone else (see Exodus 4:13). He felt positive that he could *not* do what God was asking. He was petrified to go before Pharaoh and ask him to release the Israelites. Despite his fear—the situation was dire and the pressure was on because Pharaoh was a pretty scary guy—Moses submitted to God's plan, and God enabled him to speak truth sternly to Pharaoh. Through this meek man, God did many amazing and powerful acts.

God is calling you and me to leave the bondage of our old scripts and move toward freedom. You might not feel capable of leaving your old script. I understand. I didn't think I could leave my old script either. But I found that surrendering all control to God empowers us to do more than we can imagine. Rather than making us weak, it empowers us and makes us strong and courageous. It takes greater strength to hold our tongue and act gently than it does to blurt out harsh words and ruthlessly attack. It takes more strength to rein in anger than it does to explode in rage. It takes greater strength to let go of self-protectiveness than it does to launch into defensive arguments. And it takes greater strength to apologize than it does to pass blame. But the Holy Spirit can give us this strength only as we surrender to Him by relying on God rather than ourselves.

It takes deep soul strength to surrender control and trust God in the midst of life's heartaches. When we feel powerless, we clamor after control. If you doubt that statement consider your response the next time you are falsely accused. Meekness is the vitamin E to our emotional scar tissue. Our self-protective instincts are very strong. Like scar tissue they form thick skin around our old wounds. Meekness softens the scar tissue around our old wounds and reshapes us into the image of Christ, which is, ultimately, the goal for rewriting your script. And if anyone ever provided an example of meekness it was Christ.

Looking at Our Ultimate Example

Christ's entire life was lived out in the spirit of meekness. He said, "Learn from me, for I am gentle [*praus*, the same word used for meekness in the Beatitudes] and humble in heart" (Matthew 11:29). He also said:

- "I tell you the truth, the Son can do nothing by himself; he can do only what he sees his Father doing" (John 5:19).
- "I do not accept praise from men" (John 5:41).
- "I do nothing on my own but speak just what the Father has taught me" (John 8:28).
- "I am among you as one who serves" (Luke 22:27).

The apostle Paul used Christ as an example of meekness. One reason he wrote a letter to the church at Philippi was because two women, Euodia and Syntyche, were fighting (see Philippians 4:2). Their bickering created such discord that Paul felt it necessary to give the church instructions on how to get along with each other. He pleaded with Euodia and Syntyche and the other church members to put on the attitude of Christ (in other words, to rewrite their emotional scripts). He wrote, "Do nothing out of selfish ambition or vain conceit." He continued,

> Your attitude should be the same as that of Christ Jesus: Who, being in very nature God, did not consider equality with God something to be grasped, but made himself nothing, taking

the very nature of a servant, being made in human likeness. And being found in appearance as a man, he humbled himself and became obedient to death — even death on a cross! (Philippians 2:5-8)

Let's examine this passage a bit closer and consider the choices Christ made to put on meekness.

He emptied Himself (verse 7). *Kenosis,* the Greek word translated in this passage as *empty,* expresses the idea of "setting something aside."[5] When Jesus came to earth, He didn't set aside His deity; He set aside the glory and privileges of His deity. The New King James Version says that He "made Himself of no reputation."

It's tough to set aside our reputation, particularly when we feel maligned. Our initial response is usually, "What? I've got to protect my reputation! I've got to make them apologize and clear up my name!" No, we don't. We cannot control how others view us, so we need to surrender control of this to God and take on meekness instead. That's what Christ did. He continually dealt with attacks and accusations from others, yet He didn't concern Himself with His reputation. He didn't argue to prove He was right. The prophet Isaiah wrote of Him, "He was oppressed and afflicted, yet he did not open his mouth" (Isaiah 53:7). He was the only one to ever enter this world who had every right to assert His rights, yet He waived them.

He took the position of a servant (verse 7). Instead of coming and demanding to be served, which was His rightful privilege, Jesus chose to serve (see Matthew 20:28). Instead of taking the position of honor at the Last Supper, He chose to wash the disciples' feet (see John 13).

When we hold positions of authority, we feel we deserve to be respected, and if we aren't we feel threatened and angry. Many times we'll try to work behind the scenes to get the accolades we want or to punish those who we feel are undermining us. After all, our positions demand it! We feel it is our right to be served and admired. But Jesus calls us to something different. He said those who want to be great must become servants (see Matthew 20:26).

He put on human form (verse 7). God created us in His likeness, but when Jesus came to earth, He came in our likeness. Jesus, fully God, took on human form as a baby. This is absolutely preposterous! God, the mighty Creator, became an infant baby who would need to be nursed and have His diapers changed. Could anything be more humbling? He did not come in the perfect, pre-Fall, human form. Instead, though He never sinned, He took on all the limitations of the fallen human form. This meant the God who eternally existed in endless energy became tired. The God who created time and space now willingly became bound to time and space. All the restrictions of the human body became His. He entered fully into our frailty.

He humbled Himself (verse 8). Humbling ourselves is the first step toward meekness. Biblically, humility describes "lowliness of mind."[6] It speaks of taking our rightful positions before God. Used as a verb, to humble means "to make low."[7] Keep in mind that this doesn't mean low self-esteem. It creates a picture of us bowing before God. Before we can become meek and surrender, we must bow down low, acknowledging that God knows better than we do. He is completely wise. He does not need us to tell Him how to do things or how to run His world (see Romans 11:33-36). Humility is a prerequisite to meekness.

Christ's entire earthly life was lived out in surrender to the Father's will. He consistently chose obedience to the Father's plan, even when it meant His own death on the cross. His prayer in the Garden of Gethsemane shows us that He didn't want to go to the cross, but He went willingly because that was what God had asked of Him. Jesus lamented and experienced the range of emotions, but He was submissive to the Father's desires. Rather than seeking prominence, He willingly accepted the plan the Father had ordained for Him, and that plan included a horrific death.

He submitted to the most humbling form of death (verse 8). Not only did He submit to death, He submitted to death by crucifixion. This was the most painful and shameful death that any criminal could suffer. He willingly accepted this cruel death, even though He was guilty of no crime.

What an example to live up to! How completely different from our human inclinations! But if we want to rewrite our emotional scripts and give up control, we have to have complete trust in God. Do you?

WHY GIVING UP CONTROL IS SO HARD

For many years if someone had asked me that question, I would have answered, "Yes, I trust God." In fact, I even taught others how to trust God. But when heartaches came, I often wondered if God was punishing me. I worried a lot. I put undue pressure on my adult kids to call me when they arrived at a destination to which they were driving. Sometimes I would try to talk them out of their plans—attempting to control their choices—because I felt their plans were unsafe. Even when they were away at college I lay awake at night worrying if I knew they were out driving in the middle of the night. (If I had my way, my kids would *never* drive in inclement weather.) My worries and my efforts to control what happened to those I love showed me that I did not trust God. When I came to that realization, I felt shocked. You would think someone holding a degree in biblical literature would be able to trust God. After all, I had spent four years studying His nature. But scolding myself for my lack of faith didn't help. Trying to muster up more trust didn't help either.

As I struggled to determine why, I realized that fear had become a stronghold in my life. According to Beth Moore, a stronghold is "anything that exalts itself in our minds, 'pretending' to be bigger or more powerful than our God."[8] Another author wrote, "Strongholds of fear are often constructed from the lies of the enemy and from debris left over from past hurt and abuse."[9] This was true for me. In order to protect myself from being hurt again, I had built thick walls of fear around myself. But instead of protecting me, my fears had distorted my thinking and held me captive. Just as the apostle John described, fear tormented me (see 1 John 4:18).

When I determined to rewrite my emotional script, I knew I had to design a demolition plan to knock down the stronghold of fear in my life. I wanted to trust God more than anything. My tendency to control horrified and appalled me, but the patterns I had developed over the years were entrenched in my thinking. In order to rewrite my emotional script in this area, I had to implement a demolition plan so that I could replace self-reliance with God-reliance. Let me share it with you.

A PLAN FOR DEMOLISHING STRONGHOLDS OF CONTROL

Reshape Your Thinking About the Character of God

My abuser had twisted truth in telling me that it was God's will for him to sexually abuse me. While nothing can happen to us outside of God's sovereignty, God was certainly not in favor of my abuse. In fact, it horrified Him. I had to rewrite the lies I'd grown up believing and replace them with God's life-giving truth.

For several years I studied what the Word of God taught me about His character. Rather than focusing on what my abuser taught me about God's character, I meditated on what the Bible said about God's character:

- He is good—Psalm 86:5.
- He is loving—Psalm 136:2.
- He is holy—Isaiah 6:3.
- He is faithful—Deuteronomy 7:9.
- He is gracious and slow to anger—Psalm 103:8.
- He is compassionate—Psalm 103:8.
- He is forgiving—Psalm 103:3.
- He is merciful—Ephesians 2:4.
- He is just—Deuteronomy 32:4.
- He is almighty—Isaiah 10:33.

If you need to rewrite your script in this area, compile your own list. Meditate on each truth about God's holy character, and then next to each write down why this trait provides a good reason for you to trust Him. Then thank Him for each quality. Write out a prayer of praise that is based on your list.

Recently, I looked over a list of God's attributes that I had written in my journal during a particularly difficult season of life. After the list I had written the following prayer of praise: *Abba Father, I praise You this morning. You are faithful and true. You are good and holy. You are loving and kind and Your every intention toward me is pure. Thank you that I can trust You today.* I find that the act of writing out why I can trust God helps cement this truth in my mind, thus erasing old lies and replacing them with life-giving truth. As you meditate, ask the Holy Spirit to move your knowledge of God's love and goodness from your head down into your heart.

You should also be careful not to project onto God the characteristics of those who warped your emotional script. Often little girls develop their concept of God from the image of their earthly father. (That's a lot of pressure for earthly fathers!) If your father or other significant males in your life mistreated you in some way, warping your emotional script, remind yourself *daily* that your heavenly Father is different. It may be helpful to fold a piece of paper in half. On one side list the qualities of your earthly father; on the other list the qualities of your heavenly Father. Keep this list in your Bible so that you can remind yourself often that God is completely holy. Abba Father does not warp emotional scripts; He heals them.

Release and Replace Old Patterns of Fear

I do this no matter where I am—driving my car, writing in my office, lying in bed, whenever fear creeps in and starts sending my mind into a tailspin. For example, a few days ago a gunman entered a church in our community on a Saturday night and shot and killed several young people. He escaped, but the following Sunday morning another shooting occurred at another church in our community. Late that Sunday night, as I lay in bed rehearsing the events of the day, I reminded myself that I cannot control the safety of those I love. Dwelling on what might have happened had the gunman entered our church spun off a million scenarios in my mind. So instead of playing the "what if" game, I identified my fear as from the Evil One. (He is the one who lies to me, telling me I must be in control.) I *released* my fears by mentally placing each loved one in God's big, strong hands. I reminded myself that His hands are loving, gentle, and big enough to hold my husband and children.

After releasing my fears I *replaced* them with praise and the truth of Scripture. When we rid our minds of a particular fear, it leaves an empty space that can be filled with another worry. So after I released my fear, I began praising God with Scripture: *Oh, God, I praise You that You are good. You are faithful. Your Word tells me that Your faithfulness reaches as high as the heavens. Lord, I can trust You because Your Word says that You have plans to prosper and not harm my family. Your plans for them are for good and not for evil* (see Jeremiah 29:11).

Fear has been such a stronghold in my life that I may have to release and replace many times a day. But if I am faithful, the Holy Spirit always brings my mind to rest.

Of course, God has not always protected my children in the ways that I would have chosen. On some occasions He has not kept them from getting hurt. When this happens, I am faced with a choice. Will I try to take control again or will I choose to believe that God is indeed good and that He allows things to happen that I may never understand? Will I trust that His ways are higher than mine? Will I place that child in His hands and let go?

With God's help, I am rewriting my script so that it is no longer dominated by fear and control. I need to be truthful—this has been very difficult for me. I use my demolition plan often just to be sure I don't fall back into old patterns.

DON'T QUIT; LET GO!

We are on a spiritual journey. Our goal is to rewrite our emotional scripts and be spiritually transformed. The road of spiritual growth is not easy. In some ways it's a journey out of bondage and into freedom. At times it may feel as if we are wandering in the wilderness. Right about now you might be feeling this entire journey is a little too hard. May I encourage you? Don't quit. Don't cling to the old script; let go.

Our journeys have taken us to places of desperation, places of weeping, and places of humility. By now, you may be hoping for a sense of Christ's presence. The longing within you is a good thing. Fan it, as you would a flame, so that it grows into all-consuming desire. The ache for Christ's presence will keep you going through the wilderness, and it will fill you. This is the promise of the next beatitude.

PRAYING SCRIPTURE
TO INTERNALIZE TRUTH

Holy One, the Lord Almighty is Your name (see Jeremiah 31:35). O Lord my God, how great You are! You are robed with honor and with majesty; You are dressed in a robe of light (see Psalm 104:1-2). I praise You that I can trust You because Your Word tells me that You are both sovereign and good (see Psalm 119:68). Not only are You good, but all Your ways are good. You are both loving and faithful (see Psalm 115:1). Your understanding has no limits (see Psalm 147:5). I exalt You because You are "the blessed controller of all things, the king over all kings, and the master of all masters" (1 Timothy 6:15, ph). You work out everything in conformity to Your will (see Ephesians 1:11).

Thank you that I don't need to be afraid to trust You because You are righteous through and through. Your every intention toward me is good. I never need to worry that You have ulterior or unholy motives toward me. "You love righteousness and hate wickedness" (Psalm 45:7). You hate the wrongs that have been done to me— *(name those wrongs here)* _____ —yet You promise that because You are sovereign, You can orchestrate those things for my good in my life (see Romans 8:28).

Thank you that You take great delight in me. Not only are You mighty enough to save but You are tender enough to sing over me (see Zephaniah 3:17). You love me completely. You say to me, "Though the mountains be shaken and the hills be removed, yet my unfailing love for you will not be shaken" (Isaiah 54:10). Nothing can separate me from Your love (see Romans 8:39).

Lord, based on Your character and sovereignty, I relinquish all control to You. I surrender my husband, *(insert your husband's name)* _____, my children, *(insert your children's names)* _____, and grandchildren, *(insert their names, if applicable)* _____.

I surrender my career, my plans, my hopes, and my dreams. I confess to You that I have been guilty of trying to control and manipulate *(identify specific instances)* _____.

Forgive me, Father. I acknowledge that You know what is best for my life. I surrender every area of my life to Your lordship. Holy Spirit, increase my capacity to surrender and to trust the Lord Jesus Christ. Develop in me the meekness of Christ. Bring my heart into total alignment with His. I bow before You and surrender my soul completely to You.

FURTHER TRANSFORMATION
Digging Deeper into the Scriptures

1. Memorize and meditate on Galatians 5:1 as it is written here or in another translation.

   It is for freedom that Christ has set us free. Stand firm, then, and do not let yourselves be burdened again by a yoke of slavery.

2. In your own words, write a definition of meekness here.

3. Read Genesis 3. This is the story of how sin entered our world. What evidence is there that Eve struggled with control?

4. Read Genesis 16:1-8. How do you see control issues in the life of Sarai? How did those control issues play out in her marriage? What were the consequences?

5. Read Luke 8:22-25. Describe the disciples' feelings in this situation. Reflect on the nature of Christ's power as shown here. How could Christ's power help you in a situation in which you feel powerless?

Probing Deeper into Your Emotional Script

6. Look at the list of control symptoms listed on pages 74-75. Which of these symptoms are reflected in your life? How do these symptoms of control play out in your life specifically?

7. Look over the three misconceptions about meekness listed in chapter 4. Then answer the following questions:
   a. How can putting on meekness help your self-esteem?

b. How can putting on meekness help define boundaries? Do you struggle with setting boundaries? How does meekness help clarify our boundaries?

c. Read Mark 1:35-38. How did Jesus set boundaries with the disciples?

d. One common misconception about meekness is that it makes us weak. Think about Jesus. Would you describe Him as weak or strong? Why?

8. Have you ever felt powerless? Describe how you felt here.

9. Read Proverbs 3:5-6. Is it easy for you to trust God? Why or why not?

10. Read over the plan for releasing and replacing your fears on pages 86-89. Choose one area of your life where you struggle with control. How could this plan help?

11. What tangible steps can you take this week to build your trust in God? Write about those steps here.

12. Unleash the power of praise. Read Psalm 147. List all the reasons the psalmist praises the Lord. Then write your own psalm of praise here.

CHAPTER 5

SET YOUR APPETITE ON GOD

Blessed are those who hunger and thirst for righteousness.

MATTHEW 5:6

G rowing up, Lois was a "little girl lost in the system." A product of her mother's rape, Lois was unwanted and given over to social services. She spent the first four months of her life in seventeen different foster care homes. While other babies were being cradled, fed, and tenderly nurtured, Lois was fed through a bottle that was propped up and stuck into her mouth as she lay in her crib so that no one would have to take the time to feed her.

Even after she was adopted, Lois's problems didn't end. Her adopted mother was an alcoholic and often unable to care for her. As a result of her upbringing, Lois grew up with a ravenous appetite for love, acceptance, and belonging. That appetite led her to try drugs, alcohol, sex, stripping, and unhealthy eating during her teen years. But everything she tried only magnified her hunger, and only after she completely crashed did Lois meet Jesus.

At that point, she voraciously began rewriting her emotional script. She attended Alcoholics Anonymous meetings and other recovery groups. She devoured everything she could find on the teachings of Christ and emotional healing, but still she felt something was missing. When Lois heard that I was inviting women to field-test a book about rewriting one's emotional script, she decided to give it a try. After all, what did she have to lose? She had tried every other program that promised change.

Halfway through our study, Lois realized that the deep hunger she felt for love could be the very thing God could use to redirect her appetite to Him. In the past Lois had either set her appetite on the wrong things or ignored her deep longings, hoping they would go away. Now, rather than fighting her deep hunger to be loved, Lois decided to cultivate that hunger but set her desire on Christ. As she did, huge changes began to take place in her life.

Astounded, Lois wrote me, saying:

> I have never felt so free inside and excited about my walk. My whole childhood and much of my adulthood life I lived not trusting, not belonging, and never feeling worthy. I was never able to attach to anyone or even allow them to get close. Now I have changed. I feel secure and happy in the love Christ has provided. I am okay just as I am. I do not have to perform. And, I can risk letting others become close to me. Praise God. . . . I am rewriting the script and the Holy Spirit is transforming me.

When Jesus said, "Blessed are those who hunger and thirst for righteousness, for they will be filled" (Matthew 5:6), He gave us the greatest key to emotional and spiritual transformation. Let's take a closer look at what He had in mind and at how it can transform your emotional script.

HUNGERING AND THIRSTING FOR RIGHTEOUSNESS

Jesus used *hunger* and *thirst* as metaphors that describe how we are to feel about God. These are word pictures of "intense longings that people desire to satisfy—necessities that they cannot live without."[1]

When we North Americans say we're starving, we may mean we forgot to eat lunch. When kids complain, "There's nothing to eat in this house!" they mean there are no cookies, chips, or other crunchy snacks available. But we really don't have the first clue about the hunger that millions around the world suffer and die from every day. Pastor and author John MacArthur wrote, "A starving person has a single, all-consuming passion for food and water. Nothing else has the slightest attraction or appeal; nothing else can even get his attention."[2]

Jesus chose some of the strongest desires in the natural realm to symbolize the desires He calls us to in the spiritual realm. *Hunger* and *thirst* convey desperation, continuous desperation.[3] God will bless those who *continually cultivate* a desire for more of Christ and His righteousness. This longing is to be so great that nothing else holds the same appeal. We are to be focused on one thing: knowing more of Christ and His righteousness.

Righteousness is "the character or quality of being right or just."[4] If you have been asking God to help you identify all the things that have skewed your emotional script, you may be thinking, *That's my desire—for things to be made right. I want justice!* If so, let your desire lead you to God. He is the only one who is completely holy and has a full understanding of what is right and just. So if you are craving justice and are hungry for things to be made right, let your quest lead you into God's presence.

TO HUNGER AND THIRST FOR RIGHTEOUSNESS MEANS:

I crave more and more of Christ and that I passionately pursue His presence.

David, the Old Testament writer of many psalms, understood this passion. He had one desire: to experience more of God. He longed for more of His righteousness, more of His presence, more of His heart, more of His love, and more of His joy. David's hunger for God drove him to continually seek after God's presence.

He wrote:

As the deer pants for streams of water,
* so . . .*
My soul thirsts for God, for the living God.
* When can I go and meet with God? (Psalm 42:1-2)*

O God, you are my God,
* earnestly I seek you;*
my soul thirsts for you,
* my body longs for you,*
in a dry and weary land
* where there is no water. (Psalm 63:1)*

His heart groaned, "I *must* have more of God. I will settle for nothing else." Just as a deer will die without water, David recognized that spiritually he would die without God.

This is very different from the way most of us live our lives. We desire many things: love, affirmation, success, happiness, and fulfillment, to name a few. Often this leads us on a frantic search for something we can never find. We long for an experience that fills us with joy or ecstasy, for work that brings fulfillment and purpose, for someone who can satisfy our emotional needs with love and security. These desires leave us perpetually chasing an elusive dream. As a result, God gets lost in the shuffle of our complicated lives. Some of us go an entire day, or even days, without giving Him a thought. We may not mean to neglect Him; it just happens, and then we wonder why our lives feel so empty.

If we don't satisfy our hunger with God, we will try to fill it with something else. This is particularly true when life falls apart. When life hurts, our hunger pangs feel more severe. This is when we often run to addictions — food, alcohol, spending, pleasure — in order to anesthetize the pain. Jesus invites us to surrender our addictions and to allow Him to satisfy our hunger.

This is why He called Himself the "bread of life" (John 6:35) and the "living water" (John 4:10). He is the only one who can fill the hunger of your heart. Your husband can't, even if he is Prince Charming. Your children can't, even if they are darling. Your career can't, even if it is successful and satisfying. Your money, your home, your possessions, your friends, your adventures or travel — none of these will satisfy. Only Jesus Christ can fill the ache in your soul; none other can fill it. Anything less than God Himself will leave you feeling disappointed.

Strangely, God can use a warped emotional script to give us this insight.

Our Hurts Expose Our Longing for God

At a particularly difficult time in Israel's history, the prophet Isaiah told God's people, "Though the Lord gave you adversity for food and suffering for drink, he will still be with you" (Isaiah 30:20, NLT). Adversity and suffering, hmm? Not exactly the food and drink we would choose. Yet this is the food God provided.

Why? One reason is that God sometimes allows crises to awaken in us a need for His presence. In this passage, God was longing to be gracious to Israel; He was just waiting for them to cry for help! (see Isaiah 30:19). The need to rewrite our emotional scripts can trigger in us a deeper need to be with God. Our woundedness can make us aware of our longing for Him. Notice the last phrase of what Isaiah said — "he will still be with you." Adversity and suffering make us wonder, *Where is God?* We then go looking for Him. When we become more intentional about pursuing His presence, He whispers, "I've been here all the while . . . you just haven't noticed."

Rather than stifle our hunger pangs by running from them, ignoring them, or satisfying them with cheap substitutes, Jesus invites us to bring our hunger and thirst to Him.

How Hunger for God Changes Us

Our neediness drives us into God's presence, crying, "Fix me. Fix the situation. Please God, make things right. Comfort me. Ease my pain." But as we bring our hunger and thirst to Him, our desires begin to change. No longer do we most want emotional healing. Instead, we want the Healer Himself.

This has been true for me. During the years when my life was falling apart, I began to long for God. Where was He? Had He left me? These questions propelled me into a frantic pursuit of His presence. At first, I came desperate for His healing. I pleaded, "God, I need more of You! I need You to heal me. I need You to give me wisdom. I need You to make things right." But as I began to discover the pure pleasure of His presence, I began to praise and worship Him. Instead of *Lord, make this pain go away,* I began to pray, *Lord, use this pain to develop in me a deeper hunger for You.*

God answered that prayer above and beyond what I could have imagined. I fell in love with Jesus all over again. He pulled me to Himself, and I have never felt so loved. Fear that once held me captive melted into courage. My concern that people "treat me right" was replaced with a desire to treat others right. Instead of pleading for what I desired, I began to hunger after God's heart for the world.

My thoughts began to change. Rather than *Poor me,* I began to think, *Lucky me, I get to be with the Holy One today.* My attitudes began to change. Hopelessness was replaced with hope. A negative spirit was replaced with a positive spirit. Anger gradually dissipated and joy emerged in its place. Resentment faded and forgiveness moved to the forefront.

The more I experienced God's presence, the more I longed for Him. I couldn't stop thinking about Him. I talked with Him throughout the day. Now that I have experienced Him, I can't be satisfied with anything less.

When we set our appetites on God, we lose our appetites for false substitutes. We no longer thirst as much for approval and success, because our hearts have become secure in His love. We come to realize that all along this is what we have longed for—intimacy with the Almighty. This passion for His presence is the most vital key to our transformation. That's a pretty strong statement, so in case it caught you off guard, let me explain. We can run after well-trained counselors, the best self-help books and seminars. These are all good, but they are also fallible. Only God is infallible, and He is called the Wonderful Counselor (Isaiah 9:6). Pursue Him, spend time with Him, put your effort into getting to know Him.

In the beginning, I wondered how I could pursue the presence of someone I couldn't see. Perhaps you do too. Let me offer you a few suggestions that I found helpful. I believe with all my heart that had I not made these choices, I would not be emotionally healthy today.

THE CHOICES OF A HEART HUNGRY FOR HIS PRESENCE

Each of these choices will help you to experience more of the presence of Christ and to rewrite your emotional script at the same time. It's a two-for-one deal! Each choice comes straight out of Psalm 63.

Choose to Seek Him—"O God, you are my God, earnestly I seek you" (Psalm 63:1)

Rather than running after cheap substitutes, chase after God. One of the best ways to seek Him is to read His Word, the Bible. If you don't know where to start, try the Gospels: Matthew, Mark, Luke, or John. They will give you a true picture of God through Jesus Christ. Read through the Gospels and write down your observations about Jesus Christ. Self-help books are good but they do not have the power of the living Word of God.

Another way to seek God is to talk with Him. Rather than anesthetizing your pain, running from your pain, or denying your pain, bring it to God. Tell Him how you are feeling. Be honest. Talk with Him throughout the day. Designated times of prayer are great, but I have found that I need to talk with God every few minutes. For some of you this may feel like a stretch, especially since we can't see God or audibly hear His voice. Just try it. If you begin talking with Him throughout the day, I bet you will find you are experiencing His presence.

Choose to Praise Him—"I will praise you as long as I live" (Psalm 63:4)

If you take away only one thing from this book, please let it be this: *The more we praise God, the more we want God and the more we experience His presence.* Praise awakens our hearts to God's presence (Psalm 22), and it also awakens in us a thirst for more of God.

When we choose to praise God for His character, three things happen: First, we experience more of His presence because His Word tells us that God dwells in the praises of His people (see Psalm 22:3). Second, He fills us with more desire for Himself. The more we experience God, the more we want Him. Third, when we praise Him, our eyes are drawn off our own circumstances and onto the One who is big enough to handle our circumstances. As a result, we find our moods are lifted. Our attitudes literally change because we are focused on Him and His greatness. Learning the power of praise kept me sane on days when I felt I could have completely lost my mind.

Choose to Think About Him—"I think of you through the watches of the night" (Psalm 63:6)

Remember, your thoughts have a significant impact on your emotional script. Where your mind dwells is important. If your thoughts gravitate toward worry, fear, envy, or any other kind of negative emotion, try thinking about God instead. Focus your mind on Him. For example, the next time you are facing a big project at work and your mind goes back to old messages such as "I can't do this. I'm not smart enough," instead of dwelling on those messages, think about God and how smart He is. Remind yourself about how He loves to empower you. Or the next time you feel angry and are tempted to "get even," think about God before you take any action. Ask Him what He wants you to do with your feelings of anger. When you are in bed at night and unable to sleep because worry is eating you alive, turn your thoughts to God. Thank Him that He never sleeps. Thank Him that He promises to supply all your needs. Thank Him that if He is able to keep the universe in order then He can take care of whatever you are worrying about!

We always have a choice about where our minds will camp. Paul instructs us to pitch our thought tents on the things that are true, noble, right, pure, lovely, admirable, and praiseworthy (see Philippians 4:8). The more we focus on God, the more our hunger for Him will increase.

Choose to Sing to Him — "I sing in the shadow of your wings" (Psalm 63:7)

Now you might be saying, "Seriously, Becky, I can't sing." God doesn't care. He hears in perfect pitch. I have learned the value of using worship music to enter His presence. The music prompts my praise. When the weather is gray, I fill my house with worship music and before you know it, I'm singing along. As I sing to Him my mood lifts, and I find myself filled with joy.

Choose to Cling to Him — "My soul clings to you; your right hand upholds me" (Psalm 63:8)

What are you clinging to? The bottle of alcohol, the painkillers, the bathroom scale, purging, cutting, security, wealth, success, your husband or boyfriend, your children, your counselor? What would happen if you let go and clung to God instead? It is fine to benefit from the help of others, but it is not fine to cling to them. The things we cling to other than God become idols in our lives. If you want to erase the messages of the past and embrace new, godly attitudes, you need to cling to God — and God alone.

TRANSFORMED BY OUR HUNGER FOR GOD

These choices help us pursue God's presence. Every woman I have met who becomes passionate for God's presence is slowly transformed, because we become like those we spend time with. Your heart will more easily break over the things that break the heart of God. You will become more sensitive and compassionate to the suffering around you. Your spirit will mellow as a result of your own suffering, and you will be able to enter into other people's suffering. Judgmental attitudes will be replaced with compassionate attitudes.

What will happen if you pray, "Lord, create a deeper hunger for You in my life"?

You will listen for and obey God's voice in your life. The woman who hungers after righteousness seeks His kingdom first (see Matthew 6:33). In the past you might have lived for the approval of others. Now His approval will become more important. Your heart will be tuned to listen for His instructions. The psalmist David wrote, "I will hasten and not delay to obey your commands" (Psalm 119:60). These words will become your desire. Let me give you an example of what this might look like.

Recently, my husband was studying in Starbucks. He had a lot to accomplish and very little time. As he went to the counter to put cream and sugar in his coffee, he felt the Holy Spirit prompt him to talk with a man seated at a nearby table who was reading a book called *The Jesus I Never Knew,* by Philip Yancey. Steve heard the voice of the Holy Spirit so strongly that he immediately went over to talk with this man, even though it seemed like an unreasonable request. He wondered, *Am I hearing right?* More concerned with obedience than with certainty that he was hearing correctly, Steve said, "Interesting book you are reading. What do you think of it?" His question opened a conversation that lasted several hours. As it turned out, the man was deeply discouraged, and Steve was able to encourage him. What if Steve had not obeyed?

You will wait on God for wrongs to be made right. The woman who hungers after God is willing to wait for Him to right wrongs, even when she does not understand what God is doing. Instead of charging ahead and attempting to orchestrate change, you will run into the presence of God. There He will quiet your impatient spirit and give you a "stilled and quieted . . . soul" (Psalm 131:2). As a result, you will be willing to "wait for the LORD and keep his way" (Psalm 37:34). Your old script read "impatient." Your new script will read "patient."

You will love God's Word. The woman who hungers and thirsts for righteousness craves time in the Word. She meditates and memorizes Scripture. She declares with the psalmist, "Oh, how I love your law! I meditate on it all day long" (Psalm 119:97).

My friend Judy loves the Word. She memorizes passages of Scripture so she can pray it to God. I have watched her weep her way through Psalm 91. I have knelt with her as she has praised her way through Psalm 145. She studies the Bible and meditates on what she reads. She lives, breathes, and eats the Word of God. If you ask God to create in you a deeper hunger for Him, you too will develop a deeper love for His Word.

You will "press in" to God when He seems distant. Author Dana Candler wrote about these wilderness times, saying, "The cry arises from our hearts, 'Where are You, God?' Nothing moves. No one speaks. Only quiet. Only silence. Today looks just like yesterday, empty and ordinary."[5] The woman who hungers and thirsts for righteousness understands that God's silence does not mean His abandonment. Like the prophet Isaiah, you will declare, "Though the Lord gave you adversity for food and suffering for drink, he will still be with you" (Isaiah 30:20, NLT). Instead of losing faith, like Job and David and other biblical characters who deeply desired God, you will allow adversity and suffering to send you looking for Him.

My daughter prayed, *Where are You, God?* her freshman year of college. Listen to Stefanie's words as she described what happened after she prayed that prayer:

> I felt so lonely and homesick. I kept crying out to God, longing for the comfort of His presence. I had asked Him to increase my desire for Him almost to the point of despairing. He felt so far away and I could not figure out why my prayers were going

unanswered. Finally, I realized that this *was* His answer. My barren prayers were increasing my desire for Him.

Wilderness prayers are not wasted on the Lord. Even when we do not sense His presence, He hears us. He understands our weakness (see Hebrews 4:15) and values the process of our finding strength in Him. When we cannot sense His presence, we need faith to continue, and faith pleases God. Though we feel faint, weak, or disillusioned, if we continue seeking Him, He is honored.

If you ask God for a deeper hunger, the wilderness times will not feel so scary because you will recognize that He uses such times to develop deeper longing and stronger faith.

———— ⌒ ————

Does the above describe the woman you want to become? Then take a break from reading this book. Find a quiet place where you can be alone. Kneel down and pray, *Lord, develop in me a deeper hunger for You. I want to want You, Lord. So use whatever circumstances I am walking through right now to develop in me an all-consuming passion for Your presence.*

Appetite Enhancers

Once you've prayed that prayer, you can do some things to cultivate and sustain an appetite for God. Here are a few appetite enhancers:

1. Memorize and meditate on Scripture. Center your meditation and memorization in the Psalms. In many of his psalms, David gave voice to our longings. In Psalm 119 he wrote, "My soul is consumed with longing for your laws at all times. . . . Oh, how I love your law! I meditate on it all day long. . . . How sweet are your words to my taste, sweeter than honey to my mouth!" (verses 20,97,103).

When I feel my hunger for God diminishing, I grab my Bible and begin meditating. I may focus on all the passages I have underlined.

I might read through all the verses that have dates next to them—these are specific times when God met me. I may put verses on a card and memorize them. The more I memorize and meditate, the more hungry for God I become.

2. Fast from cheap substitutes. Fasting is the self-denial of normal activities or necessities, such as food, or pleasures, such as television, in order to better focus on God. Fasting can reawaken our souls to their deepest desire: the hunger for God and His righteousness. We feel hungry for God only when we are not already full of other things. So fast in order to create some empty space to allow feelings of hunger to develop. Especially fast from those things that you use to anesthetize pain: food, alcohol, television and movies, e-mail, the Internet, novels, shopping—you know what you are prone to do when you are unhappy or bored. These things are not bad in and of themselves. But if you use them to anesthetize pain or fill too much of your time, you may be stifling your hunger for God.

3. Increase your saltiness. Salt increases our thirst. When you share Christ with others, you become the "salt of the earth" and also increase your thirst for God. Ask God for an opportunity to talk with someone about Christ. Then stay alert and look for Him to answer that prayer. My friend Jill wanted to increase her saltiness, so she began taking prayer walks around her neighborhood. As she walked past each house, she prayed for the family inside. She also prayed for opportunities to share Christ. God has answered her prayers by providing many unexpected opportunities.

OUR LONGING SATISFIED, OUR SCRIPTS TRANSFORMED

Jesus said that those who hunger and thirst for righteousness will be filled. His promise echoes what David wrote, "For he satisfies the thirsty and fills the hungry" (Psalm 107:9). God doesn't fill us once; He continually fills us. He is vast enough and wise enough to satisfy every hunger and thirst. This is the mystery of being satisfied with Christ. The more we become satisfied with Him, live in His presence, and allow Him to fill our deepest needs, the more of Him we want. This desire powerfully transforms our emotional scripts, because eventually we become like those with whom we spend time. So the more time we spend with Christ, the more our emotional responses emulate His.

I want to end this chapter with a prayer of A. W. Tozer. People called Tozer a twentieth-century prophet because he continually called Christians to a life of worship in God's presence. He was one of the most godly men in history and is the author of the classic devotional *The Pursuit of God.* As you read this prayer, make it your own.

O God, I have tasted Thy goodness,
and it has both satisfied me and made me thirsty for more.
I am painfully conscious of my need of further grace.
I am ashamed of my lack of desire.
O God, the Triune God, I want to want Thee;
I long to be filled with longing;
I thirst to be made more thirsty still.
Show me Thy glory, I pray Thee,
so that I may know Thee indeed.
Begin in mercy a new work of love within me.[6]

PRAYING SCRIPTURE
TO INTERNALIZE TRUTH

Lord Jesus, all honor and glory belong to You. You alone are righteous (see Psalm 119:137). Your righteousness exceeds my imagination. I exalt You because You are the Bread of Life (see John 6:35) and the Living Water (see John 4:10). You call to me, "Come, all you who are thirsty, come to the waters; and you who have no money, come, buy and eat" (Isaiah 55:1). You invite me to taste of You because my soul will delight in Your richness (see Isaiah 55:2). You are the only one who can truly satisfy the deepest hunger of my heart. Satisfy me in the morning with Your steadfast love, so that I will rejoice and be glad (see Psalm 90:14). Lord, I worship You because You are my portion (see Psalm 119:57). May I delight in You as my portion. Help me to taste and see that You are good (see Psalm 34:8). Lord, I praise You because You fill the hungry with good things (see Luke 1:53).

Awaken my appetite for You, Holy One. May I say with David, "O God, you are my God, earnestly I seek you; my soul thirsts for you, my body longs for you, in a dry and weary land where there is no water" (Psalm 63:1-2). "As the deer pants for streams of water, so my soul pants for you, O God. My soul thirsts for God, for the living God" (Psalm 42:1-2). Only when I learn to come to You will I be able to testify, "My soul will be satisfied as with the richest of foods" (Psalm 63:5).

God, You say in Your Word that we "do not live on bread alone but on every word that comes from the mouth of the LORD" (Deuteronomy 8:3). Holy One, increase my hunger for Your Word. Let my soul be consumed with longing for Your laws at all times (see Psalm 119:20). Your words are so sweet to my taste, they are sweeter than honey to my mouth (see Psalm 119:103). Teach me to feast on Your words. Develop within me a ravenous appetite for both Your Word and Your presence. Teach me to crave intimacy with You and to find deep joy in Your presence.

I confess that often I have filled my appetite with less than You, I have attempted to satisfy my longings with food, friends, television, alcohol, drugs, success, or (*name your particular addiction*) _____. I realize, Lord Jesus, that this addiction serves only to anesthetize pain. It cannot satisfy the deepest longings of my heart. Only You can satisfy. Fill me, precious Jesus, with a deeper longing for Yourself.

FURTHER TRANSFORMATION
Digging Deeper into the Scriptures

1. Memorize and meditate on Psalm 63:1-2 as written here or in another version. (If you are up for a challenge, memorize verses 1-8.)

> O God, you are my God,
>   earnestly I seek you;
> my soul thirsts for you,
>   my body longs for you,
> in a dry and weary land
>   where there is no water.

2. In your own words, define what it means to be hungry and thirsty for righteousness.

3. Read Psalm 119:18,45-46,97. How does meditating and memorizing Scripture increase our hunger for God and bring new freedom to our lives?

4. Read Matthew 6:16-18. Define fasting in your own words. What is our attitude supposed to be when we fast? How could this practice help increase your hunger for God?

5. Read Matthew 5:13. What did Jesus mean when He said we are to be the salt of the earth? How would it help your hunger for God if you increased your saltiness?

6. Read Psalm 34:8. Why is your hunger for God so important to rewriting your emotional script?

Probing Deeper into Your Emotional Script

7. Read Psalm 63. Think about the choices that David made. Then answer the questions below.
   a. How would your emotional script be different if you sought the Lord more intentionally?

   b. How does praising God change your attitude?

   c. How would your thought life be different if you set your thoughts on God?

d. How does worship music affect your mood?

e. What do you cling to? How would your life be different if you clung to God instead?

8. Read Isaiah 30:20. How has God used adversity and suffering to develop a deeper hunger and thirst in your heart for Himself?

9. On a scale of 1 to 10, 1 being no desire and 10 representing ravenous desire, rate your hunger for God. How is this reflected in your life and in the choices you make?

1 ————————————————————————— 10

No Desire   Ravenous Desire

10. Choose one of the appetite enhancers listed on pages 108-109 to focus on this week. Explain how this practice helped increase your hunger for God.

11. Write a prayer to the Lord, asking Him to increase your hunger for Him.

12. Unleash the power of praise. Make a list of the ways God blesses you this week. Every time you write down another blessing, stop and praise God for that particular blessing.

CHAPTER 6

EXTEND
MERCY

Blessed are the merciful.

MATTHEW 5:7

The tap on Carol's bedroom door was barely audible. When she opened it, her sixteen-year-old son collapsed into her arms. "I'm so sorry. Mommy, please don't hate me . . . don't hate me." Through broken gasps he whispered, "Kelly says she is six months pregnant. And she says . . . the kid . . . is mine."

Hayden's sobering news shattered Carol's world. Her perfect family wasn't so perfect anymore, and there was no way she could keep what her son had done a secret. While she hid her feelings from him, she didn't know how she could cope with this situation.

Growing up, Carol received the message that her family was "better" than others and that she had to excel at everything. She learned to hide mistakes, keep family secrets, and do whatever it took to look good before others. She based her worth on her performance and on being good. Without realizing it, Carol had carried those messages into her adult life. Up until Hayden's announcement, she felt good about the life she had created. She had great kids who performed well in every area of life. In one single moment all that changed, and Carol felt angry.

Over the next three months pain hit her in spasms as she battled anger, sorrow, fear, and confusion. She knew that her son was not ready to be a father. In an instant his careless decisions affected not only his life, but the life of a sixteen-year-old girl, and both their families as well.

If Hayden had been someone else's child, she likely would have looked at the parents, shaken her head, and thought, *This is your fault. Didn't you discipline your kids, teaching them right from wrong?* Months before Hayden's announcement Carol's close friend had asked her, "Do you think Hayden and his girlfriend are having sex?" Carol had immediately replied, "Absolutely not!" Smugly she had thought, *Other people's kids are having sex, but not my kid. I've raised him better than that.* But Hayden wasn't someone else's son — he was hers. She knew she couldn't let him off the hook, but she also knew he needed to know his parents loved him. She knew that if she chose to withhold mercy, the situation would only be worse. Carol had to embrace her son's girlfriend and not blame her for being half of "the problem." She had to extend mercy to Kelly's family, who was excluding Carol and her husband from many of the decisions that would affect their son's life.

Carol's desire to show mercy sent her on a journey to rewrite her emotional script. She began to reflect on how many times she had disappointed God and stood outside His door in a puddle of tears, afraid of what He would think. How many times had He extended unconditional love and mercy toward her? She told me, "How could I offer any less to my precious son?"

Indeed.

No matter how difficult it may be, Jesus calls us to extend mercy and not judgment. In the Sermon on the Mount, He said, "Blessed are the merciful, for they will be shown mercy" (Matthew 5:7).

THE TWO DIMENSIONS OF MERCY

The word translated here as *mercy* (*eleos* in the Greek) "is the outward manifestation of pity: it assumes need on the part of him who receives it, and resources adequate to meet the need on the part of him who shows it."[1] Mercy describes an active empathy that extends relief to someone in misery, pain, or distress. Mercy is more than a feeling. It is deep-seated compassion that acts to help relieve the suffering of the one in need. Paul used the same word for mercy when he described God as being "rich in mercy" (Ephesians 2:4). Paul told us that God's mercy caused Him to feel compassion for humanity's sinful suffering and to provide a way out through salvation.

TO EXTEND MERCY MEANS:

*I withhold judgment and I also take action
to alleviate the suffering of those who are hurting.*

Mercy has two dimensions. The first is *withholding judgment*, which can be very difficult for those of us who grew up with a legalistic or perfectionistic emotional script. We are quick to form judgments about people and their actions. I recently polled fifty women to find out what it is they would most likely judge in other people. The number one answer? How another mom raises her kids. A close second was how tidy a woman keeps her house or car. I suspect we do this because we are subconsciously looking to relieve some guilt of our own. It's much easier to see the fault in someone else's child than to see faults in our own. And it's much easier to see the mess in someone else's house than in our own home. Yet Jesus gave clear instructions that His followers were not to judge (see Matthew 7:1).

The second dimension of mercy is *taking action to alleviate the suffering of those who are hurting.* In Luke 10 Jesus illustrates this aspect of mercy in the story He tells about an Israelite who was assaulted and robbed as he was traveling from Jerusalem to Jericho. Several religious leaders passed by this man, who was hurt and lying in a ditch by the side of the road. Despite the man's obvious need, the Jewish leaders ignored his plight, likely because of self-centered indifference or legalistic judgmentalism. The only person to help this poor man was a Samaritan, an ethnicity despised by most Jews. Not only did the Samaritan attend to the man's injuries, he also took him to an inn and cared for him during the night. The next day he gave the innkeeper money and asked him to care for the man. The Samaritan promised to return and reimburse the innkeeper for any expenses incurred.

Jesus didn't just teach about mercy through His stories; He also lived a merciful life. While we'd expect that the perfect Son of God would spend most of His time with "good" people, He hung out with the marginalized and messy members of society: tax collectors, those struggling with addictions, the homeless, and hookers. While there are numerous examples of Jesus' mercy,[2] one of my favorites is found in John 8.

A Portrait of Mercy

Jesus is in the temple, teaching. All of a sudden there is a loud commotion, and a group of religious leaders bursts into the temple, dragging a woman they have caught in the act of adultery. They make her stand up in front of everyone, saying, "Teacher, this woman was caught in the act of adultery. In the Law Moses commanded us to stone such women. Now what do you say?" (John 8:4-5).

Can you imagine? How would you feel about being caught in such a compromising situation, and then being hauled off and publicly humiliated? We have to wonder, where was the man with whom this woman committed adultery? Did he just zip up his pants and run? Or because it was a male-dominated society did the religious leaders merely wink at his sin while focusing on hers? Either way, they cared nothing about this woman. She is nameless in the text and perhaps to them as well. In biblical times, women were seen only as objects to be used and at times abused. These men didn't bring her to Jesus because they cared about moral purity or even justice. They saw her only as a pawn they could use to trap Jesus.

The scribes and Pharisees, who were the religious leaders, had a lot of power in Jewish culture. Power often distorts people's thinking about themselves, and this certainly seems to have been the case with these leaders. Blind to their own sins, they loved to point out the sins of others. They used fear, shame, and disgrace to lord it over people. Then, as they watched Jesus' loving ministry unfold, they sensed they were losing control over the crowds and were desperate to get it back. If you trace their interaction with Jesus throughout the Gospels, you will find the scribes and Pharisees continually trying to trick and trap Him.

In this scene they were trying to ambush Jesus by quoting the Law of Moses and then asking if He agreed with the law. If Jesus condoned the stoning, He would be violating Roman law, which "stipulated that all capital punishment was a Roman prerogative, not Jewish. If Jesus agreed [with the stoning] they could accuse him to the Roman authorities."[3] If He disagreed with the Law of Moses, they could destroy His credibility. The problem is, they didn't quote the law correctly. Moses' law, written by God in the first place, required that both the adulterer and the adulteress should be put to death (see Leviticus 20:10). These arrogant church leaders brought only the woman. She must have felt terrified as she stood in the temple courts, waiting for Jesus to respond.

Let's return to the scene. After the scribes and Pharisees challenge Him, Jesus bends down and quietly begins writing in the dirt with His finger. Then He says, "Let anyone among you who is without sin be the first to throw a stone at her."

Silence. And then the sound of stones dropping, one by one, and her accusers walk away without a word. Jesus has made fools out of each of them.

Then He gently turns to the woman and asks, "Where are they? Has no one condemned you?"

In a barely audible whisper, she replies, "No one, sir."

"Then neither do I condemn you. Go now, and leave your life of sin."

Did you notice that even though Jesus alleviated this woman's suffering, He didn't let her off the hook for her sin of adultery? He specifically told her, "Go and leave your life of sin." Mercy never waters down sin. Jesus exhorted her to turn from her life of sin, but He did so without condemnation. Instead of throwing the book at her, He offered mercy. This was very different from how the religious leaders responded.

The scribes and Pharisees excelled at keeping the rules. They studied the laws God gave in the Old Testament and even added a few of their own. Their obsession with obedience led to performance-based religion and ultimately to arrogance. Looking holy to others became of paramount importance. They judged and condemned anyone who did not follow the rules as well as they did. While they may have looked good on the outside, their hearts were arrogant and judgmental. They measured theirs and others' spirituality by how well they kept the rules. They followed the letter of the law, but not the spirit of the law.

God intended the law to show each of us that no matter how hard we try, we will not measure up to His standards (see Romans 7:7). The law points out the great chasm between God's holiness and our sinfulness. Under the law, each of us is condemned, because each of us has sinned (see Romans 3:23). Under the law, each of us deserves death (see Romans 6:23), and only God's mercy enables us to escape the death we deserve. Jesus took our place and ultimately paid the price for our sin by dying on the cross. He now offers us a new script, on which is written "mercy and grace."

Mercy levels the playing field. It helps us understand that just as we have been given mercy from God, so we need to offer mercy to ourselves and to others.

Finding Your Own Script in the Story

If I were to ask you to find yourself in this story, whom would you relate to most? The woman caught in adultery or the scribes and Pharisees?

Whose script is most like your own?

If you relate to the woman, you know what it feels like to need mercy but receive none. Perhaps you are struggling with some sinful habit. Life hurts because you can't get on top of your addiction. You haven't been caught yet, but you are afraid someone will figure out your secret sin. You condemn and judge yourself harshly for your failings, and you fear that other people will see you as you see yourself, and the thought terrifies you. Your emotional script keeps you from getting close to people because they might pick up stones of judgment. It keeps you from seeking the help you so desperately need.

Perhaps your secret sin has kept you from becoming involved in a local church, especially if you've been hurt by Christians before. I understand. But be careful, because in your fear it becomes easy for you to pick up the stones and lob them at the Christians attending church, griping, "They are all so fake, and they don't care about me!" Basically, the church is filled with broken and wounded people all needing a Savior. Though it is flawed, it is still the bride of Christ, and He cherishes His bride. Perhaps you should consider attending again so that you can help make a difference by raising the church's awareness of hurting people.

Begin to cry out to Jesus like the blind beggar who called from the roadside, "Jesus, Son of David, have mercy on me!" (Luke 18:38). Jesus compassionately answered his cries with the question, "What do you want me to do for you?" (Luke 18:41). If you are caught in a hopeless situation, whether because of sin or because life feels cruel, Jesus bends down and asks you personally, "What would you like Me to do for you?"

Or maybe you relate to the scribes and Pharisees. Many of us can. Our emotional scripts read "rule follower." We keep our spiritual noses clean. We pride ourselves in being churchgoing, rule-abiding Christians. We hear on the news that yet another Christian leader has had a moral failure, and we pick up our stones, wondering how a leader can make the rest of us Christians look so bad. We hear about a gay rights parade and shake our heads in disgust and moan, "What is the world coming to?" We view gay rights and abortion rights activists as the enemy. Subconsciously, we adopt an "us versus them" attitude. We've lost sight of the person behind the label.

Yet our merciful God never does. He looks beyond the sin, into the hurting heart behind it, and offers each person who comes to Him living hope (see 1 Peter 1:3). Every time we, as Christ followers, extend mercy to someone, we reflect that living hope to the world around us, and in the process we become more like Jesus.

Moving Toward Mercy

God calls us to a life of mercy. He calls us to engage with the problems and hurts of those in our world. Religion devoid of mercy is legalism. So what can you do to rewrite your emotional script and move toward mercy?

Uproot Sinful Attitudes

As I have considered how I might move toward mercy, the Holy Spirit has shown me specific attitudes that block my ability to extend mercy and reflect hope to those around me. As you read the list of attitudes I need to confront within myself, ask the Holy Spirit to reveal pockets of this attitude within your own heart. Identifying them is the first step to uprooting them.

Self-centeredness. We're all a bit self-absorbed. We'd prefer to focus on our own personal relationships with Jesus and not worry about the rest of the world. While it's good to spend time in solitude and introspection, God wants to flow through us to others. If we focus only on our "personal walk with God," we lose the relevancy of our faith. To confront this attitude, seek the divine rhythm of solitude *and* service. Christ gave us His Spirit so that we would be the hands and feet of Jesus to the hurting world in which we live.

Judgmentalism. Jesus loves the sinner. He *loves* the sinner and calls us to follow His example. He doesn't view sinners as "the enemy."

He gave His life for them.

Years ago one of my friends decided she could no longer fight her homosexual urges. She became tired of fighting her attraction to other women and so she adopted an alternate lifestyle. I felt sad and angry and wanted to walk away from the friendship. One morning when I was on my knees in my regular worship time, Jesus spoke to me. It was as if He were standing in the room with me. He picked up a stone and handed it to me. Then He gently said, "Becky, if you are without sin, you may throw this stone." I realized that my attitude repulsed Christ. His desire is that I weep over the sin but never give up on the sinner. He was calling me to faithfully love and pray for my friend, not to judge her and push her out of my life. So instead, I intentionally chose to keep the friendship. I made time for my friend, took her to lunch, bought her birthday gifts, and prayed for her. I remind myself often that her choice to become an active lesbian was a response to great hurt in her life and that I have made sinful choices in my own life.

Where does judgmentalism crop up in your heart? One time when my husband asked a congregation to take on the problem of AIDS in a particular African nation, several people became upset. They asked, "Why are you concerned for them? It's their problem. They are sinful and deserve AIDS." How would you have responded?

When a friend confides in you that she struggles with a certain sin, do you wonder what her problem is and why she can't just stop? When you see a person holding a sign that reads, "Hungry," or someone waiting in line for a welfare check, do you jump to conclusions about his or her integrity or work ethic? When you see someone who is inebriated and lying in the street, do you feel that he deserves to be homeless because he struggles with an addiction? Oh, I wonder how often Jesus weeps because we choose judgment over mercy.

When judgmentalism creeps into your heart, confess it and counteract it by showing mercy to that person instead.

Criticism. Proverbs warns us about the damage a critical spirit can do: "Reckless words pierce like a sword, but the tongue of the wise brings healing" (Proverbs 12:18). Until we let go of criticism, we can't live merciful lives. This is particularly true in our homes, with our spouses, children, or housemates. Why is it that we are often more careless with our words with the ones we are closest to?

If your emotional script prompts you to often criticize others, ask God for a gentle tongue. It is so easy to offer continual correction when perhaps what the person needs is a hug. It's easy to use phrases like "you always" or "you never." Next time you're tempted to say those words, think about offering mercy instead. Now I know you never fight with your husband, but . . . let's suppose occasionally you do. When you feel frustrated with some action of his, instead of beginning with "you always," which causes him to erect a wall of defense, explain your feelings. Tell him what's important to you and ask if he feels he can meet you in this issue. It will transform your home and your relationship.

Indifference. Perhaps you don't judge, but you just don't get involved. You choose ignorance over being informed. Indifference is a "lack of interest or concern."[4] When we become indifferent, we no longer feel. Indifference protects us from feeling sad. It's easier to think about happy things than to focus on problems, such as world hunger. Indifference rationalizes, "What can we do about it anyway?"

Lots of Christians rationalize that they don't have to meet the needs of those in their community because that's the church's job. But I wonder, has the American church lost its mission? Instead of making a difference in the world, have churches become more focused on keeping their members happy? Is the church anything more than a religious social club? What if your church closed its doors? Would anyone in your community notice?

If you were to move, would the people in your neighborhood miss you? Have you done anything to reach out to your neighbors simply because Jesus loves them? Have you made any effort to alleviate the suffering of someone in your community?

One practical way to uproot indifference is to watch the news or read the paper with a prayerful heart. Be informed and be intentional about praying for the suffering of others. For example, let's say a story comes on the news about a murder in your community. Immediately pray for the family of the victim. Ask God for healing in their lives. Or if you are watching the news and the Palestinian conflict comes up, pray for the peace of Jerusalem.

Feeling overwhelmed. Some of us with tender hearts look at the needs all around us and become paralyzed. The sadness and the hurting in our circle of influence feel overwhelming already, so why take on other hurts? This is a natural feeling, particularly when your own family is walking through a crisis. During those times your primary focus must be those closest to you, but understand that that focus may only be for a season. Eventually you will have to reengage with the world around you because we are not called to focus only on our own families but also on the world around us.

When I become overwhelmed, I ask the Lord to sift through the many world problems and show me one I can do something about. This is what Rose did.

Rose is a young mother who became concerned about children in the foster care system. The problem felt overwhelming to her, but she began to ask God how she could get involved. She asked Him for His heart for kids in the system and became a foster mother herself. Soon God brought her a baby girl whose mother was in prison. Rose eventually adopted little Zoe and her three-year-old sister, who was in the system as well. Rose not only nurtures these two little girls, but she also takes them to visit their mother in prison. Rose has become a conduit of mercy. Rather than becoming weighed down by all the needs, she realized the impact she could have by becoming involved in two little lives.

Ask God where He would have you get involved. Start small. Become involved with one individual or one cause. Be faithful. If you dare to become a conduit of mercy, you will be amazed at how God will use you as an instrument of living hope in the lives of others.

Ask for His Heart

Mercy flows out of intimacy with God. The more we snuggle up close and feel His heart for the world, the more His heart becomes ours. Intimacy with God is more than just feeling close to Him. It's about becoming like Him. Remember, "we become like the one we worship."[5] Ask the Holy Spirit to bring your heart into alignment with His. Ask Him to allow you to see people as God sees them, even those who have hurt you.

Let me tell you about a recent answer to this prayer in my own life. While writing this chapter, I ran out to Starbucks for a quick fix. Unfortunately, my mind was on the chapter and not on driving, so I pulled into a parking space that another driver was waiting for. This is embarrassing, but I never even saw the man! When I stepped out of my car, he let me have it. He was livid and I felt awful. I apologized, but he kept ranting and raving. When I offered to move my car, he went right on fuming, so I shot up a quick prayer: *Lord Jesus, help me to see this man through Your eyes.* That's when I knew what to do. I said, "Please, sir, may I pay for your coffee?" Shocked, he began to tell me about his high blood pressure and how he shouldn't get so stressed. This man needed mercy, and I needed to pay more attention to what was going on around me!

After you ask for God's heart, be intentional about choosing to see each person as an individual. This brings me to my next suggestion.

Look Beyond the Label

I'm amazed at how quickly we label people: illegal, disabled, uneducated, pagan, liberal, conservative, criminal, and so on. Behind every label is a human being whom God loves. Find one person whose suffering you have the power to relieve. Befriend her. Focus on her individual beauty.

A few years ago I was speaking at a retreat when I met Evelyn. The day before, she had been released from jail. Initially, I wanted to ask her why she had been thrown in jail in the first place. But the Lord convicted me of this thought, and I realized I didn't need to know.

I needed to look beyond the label. So instead, I asked Evelyn to tell me about some poems she had written. Every time she finished reading a poem, she gave me another hug. I realized after hearing five poems that what Evelyn was really craving was hugs! I imagine you don't get many hugs in jail.

When I returned home from that retreat and told my kids about Evelyn, my daughter said, "Mom, I'm so proud of you for becoming friends with an ex-con!" The time I spent with Evelyn changed me. Now when I pass a prison, I realize that inside that prison are hurting people. Each person is an individual who needs mercy.

Allow Suffering and Sorrow to Soften Your Heart

In my experience, people who have had their hearts tenderized by suffering are the most merciful. Rolland and Heidi Baker would agree. As missionaries they witnessed a great revival sweep the nation of Mozambique and observed: "We found that those who are most broken, most abused, most outcast become some of the most anointed ministers we have out of thousands of churches." They went on to say that those who were suffering "run ahead in mercy" because "they know what it is to be beaten, to be raped, to be burned, cold and hungry. They're the ones who have compassion for the homeless, the broken, and for the prostitutes."[6] If you've experienced sorrow and suffering, ask God to not waste your tears. Ask Him to soften your heart through every difficult experience.

As you know, I am a breast cancer survivor. As a result, I have a heart for those who are walking through that sorrow. I also have a heart for those who have been sexually abused because that's my story as well. Lorraine has a heart for those who have had an abortion, because she had one years ago and knows the havoc that guilt can play in the life of one who's had an abortion. Debbie serves in a soup kitchen every Friday night because she remembers what it was like to be homeless for a while. Linda had an alcoholic father and feels compassion for those who struggle with the image of God as Father. Jan struggles with depression. She offers hope and healing to those who are struggling with this malaise. Just as He's done for us, God can use your sorrow to erase old messages of judgment and transform you into a woman who offers mercy and compassion to fellow sufferers.

Engage in Small Acts of Mercy

Remember, mercy is withholding judgment and also taking action to relieve someone else's suffering. Every time you take action to alleviate another's suffering, you are erasing messages of judgment from your old script and writing *mercy* there instead. For example:

- Practice being merciful to the waiter who messes up your order. You might feel frustrated but rather than allowing frustration to take over, offer understanding. Speak kindly to him and ask if he's having a stressful day. One waitress told me she had been asked how she was doing only once or twice in all the years she had been a waitress! You might even consider leaving a bigger tip in light of how stressful the job is at times.
- Offer understanding to the cashier who charges you too much. Explain that she has mischarged you. Speak kindly. Then offer some type of reassurance such as "No one gets it right all the time" or "Thanks so much for correcting the mistake. I hope the rest of your day is less stressful."
- Rather than judging the single mom whose kids have different dads, offer to help. Watch the kids one afternoon or evening a month, encourage the mom with a small gift that's just for her, or meet her for coffee and listen compassionately as she talks about her struggles.

Start small and ask God to enlarge your territory in His time.

Hang with the Hurting

If you want to develop a heart of mercy, spend time with those who are hurting. Visit a jail or homeless shelter. Rather than judging how people got there, simply offer a listening ear. A few years ago my three daughters did this. They spent a day at a homeless shelter for runaway teens. They played table tennis and pool with the kids and really just listened. They offered friendship.

Sometimes God may call you to become involved with a person long-term. You may be called on to offer friendship for many years to someone who is hurting, perhaps a friend who is walking through a messy divorce. You may need to be very faithful for years to help your friend get emotionally and spiritually back on track. These commitments can feel hard to make. Remember, God is committed to you long-term, and He may call you to emulate His mercy by modeling faithfulness in some hurting person's life.

WAYS TO HELP THE HURTING

- *Serve at a soup kitchen.*
- *Go on a short-term mission trip.*
- *Sponsor a child through Compassion International or World Vision.*
- *Volunteer at a crisis pregnancy center.*
- *Find local hangouts for the homeless and spend an afternoon listening to their stories or playing games with them.*
- *Volunteer at your local rescue mission or hospital.*
- *Read the newspaper, using it as a prayer guide.*
- *Go to the International Justice Mission website: www.ijm.org.*

The kingdom of God is for every marginalized person. Speaking prophetically about the coming Messiah, Isaiah wrote, "The LORD has anointed me to preach good news to the poor. He has sent me to bind up the brokenhearted, to proclaim freedom for the captives and release from darkness for the prisoners, to proclaim the year of the LORD's favor and the day of vengeance of our God, to comfort all who mourn" (Isaiah 61:1-2). Notice the groups for whom Jesus has a special place in His heart: the poor, the brokenhearted, the captive, the prisoner, and all those who mourn. Now the Spirit of the sovereign Lord dwells in *you*, if you are a Christ follower. He has anointed *you* to be His messenger of mercy.

What will the new merciful you look like?

THE NEW MERCIFUL YOU

As you revisit your emotional script and replace critical and judgmental attitudes with mercy, God will transform you into a woman who is:

More aware of the needs of others. I am legally blind in my left eye because of an infection I had as a little girl. The medical community can't do much for that eye. In my right eye, I have myopia (nearsightedness). A corrective lens in my good eye increases my field of vision. Mercy is like that corrective lens. It enlarges our field of vision by lifting our eyes off ourselves and helping us see the suffering of others.

If the message of your old emotional script reads, "I am alone in my pain," your new script will read, "There are others in pain." As a result, you won't feel quite so isolated. Instead, you will feel camaraderie.

More compassionate. When we choose to extend mercy, our critical feelings change to compassionate feelings — not just toward others but toward ourselves as well. Our focus changes from the sin to the hurting heart of the sinner.

More fulfilled. When we are in pain, either because of the messages in our scripts or life itself, we need a reason bigger than ourselves to get out of bed in the morning. Extending mercy to others gives us a cause. We may also feel better. Critical feelings drain us. They drag us down emotionally. On the other hand, compassionate feelings energize us. They empower us to become involved in someone else's life.

Please understand: I am not saying the reason to show mercy is so that you will feel better. It's just that when we begin to extend mercy, we get on board with one of God's purposes for our lives: to be living hope to the world around us. And that feels good.

Take some time to ask the Lord how you can be living hope to your family, friends, neighbors, and those you encounter today. Start small. Take one tiny step today toward a heart of mercy and God will bless your effort.

PRAYING SCRIPTURE
TO INTERNALIZE TRUTH

Holy One, I praise and worship You. Mercy flows from Your heart. You are rich in mercy (see Ephesians 2:4). Lord, Your great mercy and love are eternal (see Psalm 25:6). I praise You, God, my Father, because in Your great mercy You have given me new birth into a living hope (see 1 Peter 1:3).

Lord, You have invited me to pray for mercy (Hebrews 4:16). You have invited me to ask You, "What do you want me to do for you?" (Luke 18:41). I want a heart of mercy that reflects living hope to the world around me. You have said, "Blessed is he [or she] who has regard for the weak; the LORD delivers him [or her] in times of trouble" (Psalm 41:1). You have not withheld Your mercy from me (see Psalm 40:11). During the darkest times of my life, You have faithfully delivered me. In response to Your mercy, help me to "speak up for those who cannot speak for themselves, for the rights of all who are destitute" (Proverbs 31:8). You've called me to "defend the rights of the poor and needy" (Proverbs 31:9). Draw my eyes to the destitute around me: the sinner, the poor, the broken, and the needy. Tenderize my heart. Show me how to offer compassion.

Lord Jesus, You have said, "Do not judge, and you will not be judged. Do not condemn, and you will not be condemned" (Luke 6:37). Lord, I confess to You that it is so easy for me to judge and condemn. Show me how to rewrite the script and offer mercy instead. Help me today not to look at the speck of sawdust in my brother or sister's eye (see Luke 6:41). Instead, show me how to see clearly, by removing the plank from my own eye, so that I might be able to offer mercy.

Holy Healer, continue to heal the hurting places in my heart so that I might be able to offer comfort to others who are also hurting. Your desire is for me to get on board with Your mission of binding up the brokenhearted, proclaiming freedom for captives and "release from darkness for the prisoner," and proclaiming the year of the Lord's favor.

To bestow on them a crown of beauty instead of ashes, the oil of gladness instead of mourning, and a garment of praise instead of a spirit of despair (see Isaiah 61:1-3). I praise You, Lord of mercy, that today You will do this through me.

FURTHER TRANSFORMATION

Digging Deeper into the Scriptures

1. Meditate on and memorize Micah 6:8 as written here or in another translation.

   He has showed you, O man, what is good. And what does the LORD require of you? To act justly and to love mercy and to walk humbly with your God.

2. Define *mercy* in your own words.

3. How would you describe the difference between mercy and compassion?

4. Read Luke 18:35-43. How did Jesus demonstrate mercy in this story? If Jesus were to bend down and ask you, "What do you want Me to do for you?" how would you respond?

5. Read Matthew 7:1-5. Why do you think Jesus feels so strongly about our judging one another? Why do you think it is so easy for us to fall into patterns of judgmentalism?

6. Do you think mercy is at odds with justice? Why or why not?

7. Read Mark 15:33-41. This passage describes Jesus' crucifixion. Reflect on the scene. How do justice and mercy meet at the Cross?

Probing Deeper into Your Emotional Script

8. What messages were written in your emotional script about rule following? How have these messages influenced your ability to extend mercy?

9. Read John 8:1-11. Spend some time reflecting on the story. Read it several times if it helps. With whom can you relate best? Why? What has God spoken to you personally through this story?

10. Read Isaiah 30:18. How has God been gracious to you? Write about that here.

11. Read over the attitudes listed in chapter 6 that need to be uprooted for us to move toward mercy (see pages 124-127). With which attitude do you struggle most? What can you do this week to rewrite the script and uproot that attitude?

12. Unleash the power of praise. Read Psalm 116:1-2,5. Write all the ways God has heard your cry for mercy and all the evidences that you have seen that He is full of compassion. Then spend time praising Him for His mercy and compassion in your life.

CHAPTER 7

UPROOT GENERATIONAL SIN

Blessed are the pure in heart.

MATTHEW 5:8

"**B**ecky, how could this have happened?" My heart froze as I listened quietly to Rena confess that she had been having an affair.

I had been meeting with Rena for months. From all appearances, she was working hard and making progress on rewriting her emotional script. Our conversations often revolved around pursuing God's presence. So how could this have happened?

The more I explored this with Rena, I realized we had overlooked something significant in her life. When Rena was twelve years old, her mother had had an affair. No one in her family had talked about it. In fact, one time when Rena brought up the affair, she was told to just forgive her mother. Now Rena was committing the same sin.

While Rena was not an "innocent victim" of her mother's sin—she had made her own choices—she had failed to realize that the sins of the fathers and mothers are often passed on to their children (see Exodus 20:5). For her to salvage her marriage and rewrite her emotional script, she needed more than mentoring from me, she also needed counseling from a well-trained, godly professional who could help her uproot the sins of her parents.

Like Rena, many people unwittingly pick up the torch of sinful patterns. Left unaddressed, sins such as bitterness, anxiety, lying, addictive behavior, and sexual immorality often show up in the next generation and have an impact on our emotional scripts. In fact, it's possible to be passionate about God, spend time with Him regularly, and still be susceptible to temptation and sin, particularly if we haven't dealt with the lingering messages of our emotional scripts or uprooted the sins of our parents. I believe that's why Jesus gave us this next beatitude: "Blessed are the pure in heart, for they will see God" (Matthew 5:8).

CLEAN HEARTS

Pure is a translation of the Greek word *katharos,* which means "being cleansed."[1] When Jesus spoke of the "pure in heart," He was referring to those whose hearts had been or are in the process of being cleansed.

TO BE PURE IN HEART MEANS:

I continually uproot the sin in my life,
even generational sin.

All of us make sinful choices, even after we have recognized how desperate we are and have asked for God's forgiveness, even after we have set our appetites on God and have committed to extend mercy. Jesus understands how vulnerable we are to sin and how easy it is for us to excuse it, particularly those sins that are deeply rooted in our emotional scripts. The only way to become who we really are in Christ is to pull sin up by the root. If we don't, that same sin will keep reappearing in our lives.

When Steve and I first married, we had a garden. Neither of us knew much about tending a garden, so we didn't stay on top of the weeding. One day he looked out the window and saw that the weeds were tall and noticeable. Since we lived in a farming community at the time, Steve didn't want the neighboring farmers to think that their pastor couldn't garden, so he chose the quickest solution to the problem: He mowed our garden. The next day it looked much better, but that didn't last. Because he had not pulled up the weeds by the roots, it took only a few days for all the weeds to grow back. In fact, they seemed to have multiplied!

The heart is like a garden, and something similar can happen with our emotional scripts. If we don't pull out the generational sins in our emotional scripts, the sins of previous generations will crop up in our own lives, strangling all the progress we may have made.

---

*Generational sin is a sinful pattern
that is passed down from one generation to the next.*

Understanding Generational Sin

Author M. Scott Peck wrote, "To come to terms with evil in one's parentage is perhaps the most difficult and painful psychological task a human being can be called on to face. Most fail and so remain its victims."[2] We see this principle played out in a story found in Genesis 20.

Abraham, the godly patriarch, moved to the town of Gerar with his beautiful wife, Sarah. She was so gorgeous that Abraham felt nervous that the men of the town would kill him so that they could have her. So, in an effort to protect himself, he lied and told the people of the town that Sarah was his sister. Everything was going well until the king, Abimelech, found himself attracted to Sarah and brought her to his home to pursue a sexual relationship with her. But God did not let Abimelech touch Sarah. Instead, He spoke to Abimelech in a dream, telling him that he was as good as dead because he had taken Abraham's wife (see Genesis 20:3). Needless to say, Abimelech quickly gave Sarah back to Abraham.

Now fast-forward a few years. Abraham's son Isaac is in the same town of Gerar (see Genesis 26:1-7). The men of the town can't help but notice that Isaac's wife, Rebekah, is beautiful. Isaac gets nervous, just like dear old dad, and lies, saying, "She is my sister" (26:7), just like dear old dad. Everything went along smoothly for Isaac until Abimelech (yes, the very same king!) looks out his window and sees Isaac caressing Rebekah. Abimelech gets ticked off and he challenges Isaac, saying, "She is really your wife!" Isaac confesses that he was scared and so he lied.

Where had Isaac learned to lie to save his own skin? Yep. From dear old dad. The sin of lying had been passed down from one generation to the next.

In her book *From Fear to Freedom,* Rose Marie Miller wrote about the bitterness her mother had toward her father because he had invested all their money in the stock market before the 1929 crash. Miller said, "I did not then see the parallel between my mother's becoming bitter toward Dad and my becoming bitter toward Jack [her husband]. But it should be clear that parental examples are powerful. The sins of the generations are handed on to the children, and often unconsciously, the children receive them without understanding they are inheriting."[3] Just as lying was handed down to Isaac from Abraham, bitterness was handed down to Rose Marie from her mother.

Unless we uproot the generational sins in our emotional scripts we will likely repeat the sinful patterns of the previous generations. So how do we uproot generational sin? We reflect, repent, and make restitution.

Uprooting Generational Sin
Let's start with reflecting, which is a two-step process.

Step 1: Examine your family tree.

To live a pure life and to leave a pure legacy (which we will talk about more specifically in chapter 10), we must break all ties with any generational sins in our family trees. The apostle Paul counseled how to do this: "Rather, we have renounced secret and shameful ways; we do not use deception, nor do we distort the word of God" (2 Corinthians 4:2). The word Paul used here for *renounce* means not only to speak out against but also to "disown."[4] We don't disown our families, but we do need to disown the sins of our families. When we break our ties with those sins, we break the cycle of handing them down to the next generation.

In *Finding Calm in Life's Chaos* I listed four questions that flow out of this verse.[5] I repeat them here because they can help you uncover any lies you may have believed and determine whether there are specific sins that you need to renounce.

1. What are the secrets of my family? Paul wrote that we are to renounce "secret" ways. When you are trying to figure out the generational sins in your family history, start by looking for addictions, events, or behaviors that no one ever talks about. It may feel scary or disloyal to explore the secrets of your family tree, particularly if you have grown up with such messages as "We don't need to share our dirty laundry with the world." If so, ask God to give you the courage to uncover the truth. Remember, secrecy is almost always a red flag that there is sin involved.

One way to identify family secrets is to think back on the stories you heard growing up. My friend Jill remembers hearing about how her mother was sent to the local bar at nine years of age to rescue her drunk grandfather and help him home. So it wasn't hard for Jill to figure out that her grandfather was an alcoholic, even though no one ever talked about it.

Another way to figure out the family secrets is to carefully ask a few questions. For example, you might ask your parents or grandparents:

- Has anyone in our family struggled with addictions? If so, which ones? (Addictions are tricky. They have a genetic component but usually start with sinful choices.)
- Has there ever been a suicide or suicidal attempt in our family? (Suicide and suicidal attempts are extremely generational.)
- Is anyone in our family not speaking to or cut off from anyone else in the family? If so, why?
- Have there been any unwanted pregnancies or abortions?
- Has anyone in our family practiced witchcraft or been involved in the occult?

Talk also with your siblings. How do they remember your childhood? What topics were taboo? It might even be helpful to draw a family tree and list secrets associated with each relative.

If you want to rewrite your script, you need to dump the rule that says, "Don't tell." The only way to not repeat patterns is to bring the truth into the open.

2. Are there any shameful ways in my family? "Shameful ways" are patterns of sin that produce shame, for example, sexual abuse, spiritual abuse, words intended to embarrass or make a person feel ashamed or guilty, suicidal attempts by family members, addictions to pornography, and any other behaviors that might bring shame on a family. (Even though we talked about addictions in the first question, they could also be looked at here.) Trace through your family tree. Identify the shameful ways in your family.

3. Are there patterns of deception in my family tree? Children raised in homes where lying to get out of a tough situation was acceptable often lie to get out of sticky situations as adults. But deception can go beyond lying.

Deceptive patterns manifest themselves in a pronounced need to protect a public image that does not match who the person is in private. Deceptive patterns can show up in an intolerance of criticism, so the person refuses to see himself as sinful and adopts an attitude of denial. They can also show up in an obsession with appearing spiritual. As a result, those at fault never accept responsibility for their actions.

4. Has my family distorted the truth found in God's Word? For example, Scripture clearly says that children are to be disciplined in love (see Ephesians 6:4), yet some Christian parents rely too heavily on spanking as a form of discipline, at times even leaving bruises on their children. They justify their actions by quoting the adage, "Spare the rod and spoil the child" (see Proverbs 13:24). This is a distortion of Scripture. God never intended beating as a form of discipline. Children who grow up with violence in their homes often repeat the pattern.

I realize that the subject of spanking is controversial. Personally, I don't feel this verse implies a literal rod. I believe the author, Solomon, is speaking poetically of how important godly discipline is in the life of a child. I challenge you to search the Scriptures and search your childhood. Analyze how you were disciplined and whether the discipline encouraged you toward godliness. If you struggle with anger, be very careful when disciplining your children. If you have spanked out of anger, apologize to your child.

Suppose that through this process you discover there have been patterns of deception in your family. Uncle George cheated on last year's income taxes, Aunt Martha lied in an effort to cover up a premarital pregnancy, and your own mother shades the truth whenever she's in a jam. Write out each pattern of deception that you have discovered, and then begin to examine your own life.

Step 2: Examine yourself.

The goal of self-examination is to figure out which sinful patterns you have inherited. To do this, get alone with God and bring the list that you have compiled from asking the questions above. Ask the Holy Spirit to direct you as you do some soul searching. Ask Him to help you discern what impact those patterns of deception have had on you and your emotional script. Pray like David, "Search me, O God, and know my heart; test me and know my anxious thoughts. See if there is any offensive way in me, and lead me in the way everlasting" (Psalm 139:23-24). Then ask yourself these questions:

- Do I engage in any of the secretive behavior I saw in my family history or any other secretive or self-destructive behavior?
- Am I feeling ashamed or guilty? If so, for what?
- Do I twist or exaggerate the truth or withhold information in an effort to cover up the truth? Am I honest when filling out my income tax forms? Do I faithfully file to pay taxes? Have I lied to any of my children when asked about my sexual activity before I was married?

After you have answered these questions, you may discover that you shade the truth. For instance, someone calls, asking to speak to your husband who is home but doesn't feel like talking on the phone, and you say that he isn't home. Or you slant the truth on your income taxes so you won't have to pay quite as much. Write down any instance you can think of when you have been guilty of shading truth.

Once you have reflected on your family tree and your own life, you are ready to take the next step in uprooting generational sin.

Repent

Repentance begins when we agree with God that our wrongdoing is sin. If you have discovered that you lie to get out of jams or that you have cheated the government by shading the truth on your income tax forms, come before God, saying, *Lord, I have sinned. I need Your forgiveness.* This is what it means to confess sin. When we confess our sins to God, He forgives us and cleanses us (see 1 John 1:9).

There are times when it is beneficial to confess not only to God but also to someone else, such as a spiritual adviser, godly counselor, small-group leader, or close friend (see James 5:16). This can provide the accountability needed to denounce a particular sin. At times, for the sake of reconciliation, which we will talk about in the next chapter, you will need to confess your sin to those whom you have hurt. Confession not only cleanses our hearts, but also sets us on the path toward change. It's not enough to merely confess our sin. We must also make a deliberate choice to move away from that sin. This is what it means to repent.

The word *repentance* is from the Greek word *metanoeo,* which means "to change one's mind or purpose."[6] Repentance is a choice to turn from sin, and it is to be a *daily* pattern in the life of the believer. Repentance keeps our hearts pure and pliable before the Holy Spirit.

Sometimes we develop an emotional attachment to certain sins. In order to extricate ourselves emotionally from that sin, we must first confess it and then choose repentance. If we wait until we *feel* sorrow for the sin, we might never repent because some sins *feel* good—at least initially. For example, it might feel much easier to lie to get out of a jam than admitting the truth that you've become an expert in rationalization. If you are not paying your taxes or lying on your income tax form, you might rationalize, thinking, *Well, I don't like what the government is doing with my money anyway.* Or if your child asks you if you had extramarital sex, you lie, telling yourself, *I don't want to be a bad example.* In other words, it's become emotionally comfortable for you to lie to get out of a jam. You've become so comfortable with lying that you don't even know when you're doing it.

If the Holy Spirit has revealed that this is the case about a particular sin in your life, ask God to give you godly sorrow (see 2 Corinthians 7:10) for that sin. Godly sorrow is *sadness* that our sin has grieved God; it is *not* regret that you've been caught or exposed. Let me explain.

We live on a golf course and this provides constant temptation for our dog, Maverick, a very emotionally needy goldendoodle. He watches the golfers with envy and longs to join in the fun, so we put up an electric fence to keep him contained. One day, however, temptation got the best of him. Maverick watched a golfer take his best shot, charged through his electric fence, retrieved a ball off the green on the fourth hole, and brought it back to the golfer's feet. He then sat panting, waiting for a "good boy." Instead, what he received was a severe scolding from my husband. Steve walked Maverick back and forth across the electric fence to remind him of the consequences of running away. Maverick hasn't broken through the electric fence since. But does that mean Maverick experienced godly sorrow? Not a chance! If we unplugged his fence, he'd be back out there in a minute, playing with the golfers.

Some of us are like Maverick. We regret only the "shock" that comes with getting caught. We regret our sin because of the consequences. But we never experience godly sorrow over that sin. We'd do the same thing all over again if we could get away with it. That is not true repentance.

When we have godly sorrow, our emotions align with God's over the sin. Beth Moore wrote, "Godly sorrow is a change of heart resulting in complete agreement with God over the matter. The change in our feelings will come from a change in our hearts."[7] Sometimes sorrow leads to repentance, but other times we need to ask the Holy Spirit to give us feelings of sorrow over our sins, even though we have already repented.

I believe it is also wise to ask God for godly sorrow over the sins committed by our parents and grandparents. If we are going to make a break with the sinful patterns in our family trees, we need to feel as God feels about those sins. We may even weep on behalf of the sins of previous generations. This is what the Old Testament prophet Ezra did. When he realized the extent of the sin of God's people, he fell on his face before the Lord and cried out, saying, "O my God, I am too ashamed and disgraced to lift up my face to you. . . . From the days of our forefathers until now, our guilt has been great. Because of our sins, we . . . have been subjected to the sword and captivity" (Ezra 9:6-7).

If you are in captivity because of the sins of your grandparents and parents, cry out to God. Godly sorrow will help you renounce those sins and detach yourself from the curse of those sinful patterns.

One way to develop godly sorrow is to explore what God's Word has to say about the particular sin with which you are struggling or with which your ancestors struggled. For instance, if your family has patterns of deception, as we have been talking about, use a concordance and look up what God says about lying. Then ask Him to help you feel about deception as He feels. It may even be helpful to gather two or three friends who know you well and ask them to pray that the Holy Spirit would develop godly sorrow in you and uproot any trace of deception from your emotional script.

When you repent of a sin, write about it in your journal, being sure to note the date. This will crystallize the repentance in your mind.

The last step in uprooting generational sin is making restitution. When you have sinned against someone or your sin has hurt someone, you need to make things right between you and that person.

MAKE RESTITUTION

Restitution begins with an apology, admittance of wrongdoing, and a request for forgiveness from the person you have hurt. If you have lied to a friend to get out of a jam, go to that friend and ask for her forgiveness. If you have shaded the truth with your kids, go to them and apologize and ask for their forgiveness.

Sometimes we have to do more than apologize and request forgiveness. There are times when we need to make amends. The word *amends* means "compensation for a loss or injury."

When we make amends with those we have hurt, we are more likely to have our relationships with them restored. We see an example of this in Scripture. The apostle Paul helped Onesimus, Philemon's slave, make amends with his owner by writing a letter to Philemon. Before he was a Christ follower, Onesimus had wronged his owner, perhaps by running away. In his letter, Paul offers to pay Philemon for any debt Onesimus might owe him (Philemon 18), likely because the former slave did not have the resources to pay back the debt himself.

Because Paul helped Onesimus make amends, his relationship with Philemon was restored.

After you have apologized and asked for forgiveness for hurting someone, prayerfully consider doing something to make things right with that person. For example, if your children have been hurt through your lying, you might make amends by paying for them to see a counselor so that they get the help they need to heal. If you have cheated a fellow business partner, pay that person back; if you cheated on your income taxes, pay back what you owe.

After you have reflected, repented, and made restitution, you need to make a plan for how to deal with future temptation.

Make a Plan to Deal with Future Temptation

Even after we have identified and repented of the generational sins in our lives, we will still be tempted to commit those sins in the future. Think about it: If the Son of God was tempted (see Matthew 4:1), what makes us think we won't be? Scripture tells us that while He was here on earth, Jesus experienced every temptation we have ever experienced yet without sin (see Hebrews 4:15).

The Bible teaches us that temptation comes from two places: from Satan and from our own desires. When Satan tempts us, we are to resist him (see James 4:7). One way to do this is by putting on the armor of God and learning to use His sword, which is the Word of God. Throughout this book I have reminded you to fill your mind with Scripture. That way when Satan starts with his "blah, blah, blah," you can slay him with Scripture. Satan is a liar, Scripture is truth. I know I risk sounding like a broken record, but I believe there is nothing more critical to rewriting your emotional script than to use the sword of Scripture.

Our desires can also tempt us. James wrote, "Temptation comes from our own desires, which entice us and drag us away" (James 1:14, NLT). Our desires represent what we want, whether good or bad. They are often birthed in our skewed emotional scripts. While our desires may not be wrong (such as the desire for love, affirmation, success, or friendship), they may tempt us to sin. Here are some examples of what this can look like:

- Deseree craves affection. That desire is good and healthy. The problem comes when her desire for attention becomes so overwhelming that she flirts with married men to receive that attention.
- Maureen desires recognition and affirmation. Again, her desires are not wrong. But temptation comes for Maureen when her boss asks her to do something unethical. Maureen falls into sin when her desire for a promotion gets in the way of her ethics.

Because our desires can tempt us to sin, we need to keep close watch on them. Our desires can feel very powerful, particularly when they arise out of needs that were not met during our childhoods. It is important that we don't deny that we have those desires because denial is a form of lying, and we are trying to uproot deception.

So acknowledge your desires, then bring those desires to God. You might pray something like this: *Lord, I really want that promotion at work. I feel so down on myself and that promotion would feel so validating. But, Lord, You have already validated me. You tell me I'm precious and important to You. Lord, help me not to sacrifice my convictions to get that promotion. I surrender my desire to You.*

Let's go back to the sin we've been using as an example: lying or deceiving. If you have found yourself following family patterns of deception, it will help if you know the types of situations where you will most likely be tempted to lie. Perhaps you sometimes lie to get out of a dinner engagement you don't want to attend. Or maybe you lie whenever you are backed into a corner about some wrongdoing. Your self-protective instincts are so strong that rather than admitting wrong-doing, you'd rather lie.

If you prepare yourself for those situations, it will increase your ability to resist the temptation. For example, if you have cheated on your taxes in the past, this tax season find someone to help you. It might even be worth hiring an accountant so you are not tempted to cheat. Another idea is to wear a wristband for a while, and every time it catches your eye, remind yourself that you are committed to telling the truth.

We also need to watch our self-talk. Everyone talks to herself internally. What you say to yourself is important because it shapes your thinking. Let's suppose that your husband is currently traveling a lot and not meeting your emotional needs. You want more of his affection and attention. How you talk to yourself will influence the purity of your choices. If you tell yourself, "My husband is never around. He doesn't make time for me. I deserve better than this," it won't be long before you will feel justified setting your desires on the cute worship leader at church or the hot barista at Starbucks, particularly if he is attentive. However, if you tell yourself the truth: "My husband is extremely busy. We need to sit down and talk about how we are going to manage our schedules and how each of us is going to be more intentional at filling each other's emotional needs," you'll be more likely to keep your wedding vows. (It's a good idea to carry your wedding vows in your wallet. That way they are readily available for a quick reminder of what you promised before God.) Most affairs and divorces start in the mind. The conversations we have in our heads are critical. Instead of dwelling on the negative feelings, surrender them and refocus. Buy your husband a gift, call a friend, take a walk, write a card of encouragement — anything to redirect your mind.

In addition, it is important to have a few close friends with whom we are open and honest. Some call these friends "accountability partners." I don't really like that term because it sounds a bit like a business partnership, but I like the idea of being so close with people that you give them permission and even invite them to have a voice in your life. I have several friends who can ask me anything, and I will be open and honest with them, because I know they love me.

Temptation will come. If you teach yourself to keep a close watch on your desires, be honest about what you are feeling, guard your self-talk, and find the courage to tell at least one other godly person, the gravity of temptation's pull will decrease.

STAND STRONG

If you have followed each step listed in this chapter, you are experiencing new freedom and your emotional script is changing. Isn't it great to know that you don't have to live in bondage to the sins handed down to you? By rewriting your emotional script, you will be breaking the cycle of generational sin. But let me warn you that Satan wants you back in bondage, and he wants those coming up behind you in bondage. In addition to rewriting your script, begin praying now that your children will not fall into generational patterns of sin. Stand strong!

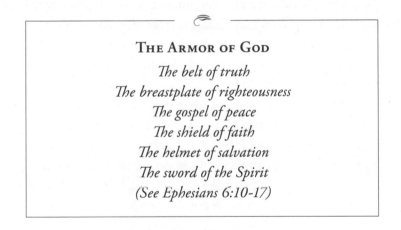

THE ARMOR OF GOD

The belt of truth
The breastplate of righteousness
The gospel of peace
The shield of faith
The helmet of salvation
The sword of the Spirit
(See Ephesians 6:10-17)

I want to end this chapter with Paul's words. As I am writing this, I am praying this as a prayer of blessing over you: "Be strong in the Lord and in his mighty power. Put on the full armor of God[8] so that you can take your stand against the devil's schemes" (Ephesians 6:10-11).

PRAYING SCRIPTURE
TO INTERNALIZE TRUTH

Lord, I worship You because You are holy. Your holiness is beyond my ability to grasp. I praise You, Lord. I ascribe to You the glory due Your name; I worship You in the splendor of Your holiness (see Psalm 29:2). I cry out with the psalmist, "Praise the LORD from the heavens, praise him in the heights above. Praise him, all his angels, praise him, all his heavenly hosts" (Psalm 148:1-2).

"Create in me a pure heart, O God, and renew a steadfast spirit within me. . . . According to your unfailing love; according to your great compassion blot out my transgressions. Wash away all my iniquity and cleanse me from my sin" (Psalm 51:10,1-2). Break any ties I might have toward the generational sins of my family. Lord, You desire truth in the inner parts; teach me to face honestly my tendency toward sin. You have searched me and You know me. You know where I am prone to sin. You perceive my thoughts from afar. Before a word is on my tongue, You know it completely. You understand me better than I understand myself, so search me, Holy Spirit, and show me any sinful area of my life (see Psalm 139:1-2,4,23).

You have promised, O Lord, that if I cry out to You, You will sprinkle clean water on me, and I will be clean; You will cleanse me from all my impurities and from all my idols. You have promised me a new heart and a new spirit. You will remove my heart of stone and give to me a new heart of flesh (see Ezekiel 36:25-26). Lord, I want that new heart. If I confess my sins, You are faithful and just to forgive me all my sins and cleanse me from all unrighteousness (see 1 John 1:9).

Father, set me free from the bonds of generational sins. Lord, I ask for forgiveness and freedom from legalism, dishonesty, denial, sexual infidelity, selfishness, unforgiveness, bitterness, and any other sin passed down to me from previous generations. I ask for freedom from witchcraft or occult practices that might have impacted my life. Your Word tells me, "Fathers shall not be put to death for their children, nor children put to death for their fathers; each is to die for his own sin" (Deuteronomy 24:16). While I know I will not be held responsible for the sins of my parents, free me from the tendency toward those sins and from the effect of those sins. I praise You that Your Word declares that if I am in Christ, I am a new creature, "the old has gone, the new has come!" (2 Corinthians 5:17). I praise You for the cleansing power of Your blood.

FURTHER TRANSFORMATION
Digging Deeper into the Scriptures

1. Meditate on and memorize 2 Corinthians 4:2 as written here or in another translation.

   Rather, we have renounced secret and shameful ways; we do not use deception, nor do we distort that word of God.

2. Define generational sin in your own words.

3. Read Romans 5:12-13,18. According to these verses, where did generational sin begin? If sin entered the world through one man's choice, why are we all accountable for sin? What is the hope found in verse 18?

4. Read Ezekiel 18:19-20. What do these verses teach us about generational sin?

5. Read Romans 6:11,14,18. What principles do you find in these three verses that can help you in your battle with sin?

6. Read Romans 7:18-19. Paul described here his own struggle with sin. Can you relate to Paul's feelings? Describe a time when you felt this way about your own battle with sin.

7. Read Romans 8:5-6. What does it mean to set your mind on what the Spirit wants? Describe how your life would look different if your mind was controlled by the Holy Spirit.

Probing Deeper into Your Emotional Script

8. Examine your family. Draw a family tree. Then answer the four questions listed below:

   a. What are the secrets of my family?

   b. Are there any shameful ways in my family?

   c. Are there patterns of deception that keep showing up in my family?

   d. Has my family distorted truth found in the Bible?

9. Now examine yourself. What sinful patterns have you internalized that came from your family?

10. Read Psalm 51. Write a prayer to the Lord confessing your sins. In your prayer, ask God for godly sorrow over those specific sins.

11. Read Ephesians 6:10-18. In this passage Paul wrote about putting on the armor of God. How could putting on this armor help you break the patterns of generational sin in your life?

12. Unleash the power of praise. Take a walk. Spend time on your walk praising God that He has cleansed you from all sin.

CHAPTER 8

FORGIVE YOUR OFFENDERS

Blessed are the peacemakers.

MATTHEW 5:9

"Becky, you must forgive."

If someone had told me that I needed to jump off a cliff or take up bungee jumping, I couldn't have been more stunned. I stammered out, "But . . . I think . . . I already have. . . ."

There was a long pause, and then the speaker said, "No, I don't think you have. I can see fear written all over your face. If you want to be set free from fear, you must forgive."

I had come so far in rewriting my emotional script. Was fear still that evident?

I swallowed, trying to choke back tears. Then I whispered, "How? How do I do that?"

Another long pause. Then, "Begin by going back to every memory you have of being abused. As you revisit each incident, tell God you are willing to forgive."

I bit my lip and tears streamed down my face. My throat closed and my stomach felt nauseated. "You don't know what you are asking me. I have already visited those memories. I cannot go back. Is there another way?"

For the past year the Holy Spirit had been prompting me to tell a particular Christian leader about the sexual abuse I had experienced growing up. I figured it must be my imagination, because I had never met this person, but the promptings continued. Then one Sunday my husband and I visited another church in town. Imagine my shock when we entered the sanctuary and this man was the guest speaker! Sure enough, throughout the service the Holy Spirit nudged me to talk with him, and since I could no longer deny the promptings, I silently told the Holy Spirit I would obey. After I told this Christian leader my story, he invited both Steve and me to have coffee with him, and that's when he challenged me to forgive the person who had abused me as a child.

The next morning, after my family had left the house, I lay face-down on my bedroom floor and told the Lord that I wanted to forgive but that I didn't know how. I began to pray, *Holy Spirit, I am petrified of revisiting those horrible moments, but if You will lead me, I will follow You even there.*

The Holy Spirit was more than willing. It was as if He led me down a long, dark corridor, opening door after door. Behind each door, I saw a little girl being sexually abused. She tried to scream for help, but no sounds came out of her mouth. As I watched each scene, I felt angry, sad, afraid, powerless, confused . . . and a host of other emotions.

Each time I watched another episode of abuse, the Holy Spirit whispered, "Becky, will you dare to give Me your hurt? Your pain? Your anger and your fear? Will you forgive?"

Between broken sobs, I whispered, "Yes." When I was finished four hours later, I felt exhausted but also free from fear and anger.

That day was the beginning of my journey to forgive the one who had abused me. Yes, it was only the beginning. For years I had resisted forgiving the person who had done such evil toward me, yet I knew that if I wanted to move ahead emotionally and spiritually, I had to take this step. Forgiving my abuser has not been simple, nor easy. Indeed, it has been gut-wrenching. Sometimes I feel I have completed the journey, and then the Holy Spirit reveals another layer of anger or resentment tied to the abuse. Once again, I must affirm my decision to forgive.

Most of us have been hurt or angered by significant people in our lives—our parents, a teacher, a pastor or youth leader, a relative, a boss or coworker, or a friend. God calls us to forgive these people. Jesus said, "For if you forgive men when they sin against you, your heavenly Father will also forgive you. But if you do not forgive men their sins, your Father will not forgive your sins" (Matthew 6:14-15). When Peter asked, "How many times shall I forgive my brother when he sins against me?" Jesus responded, "I tell you, not seven times, but seventy-seven times" (Matthew 18:21-22). Jesus was saying that even if someone repeatedly hurts us, we keep on forgiving that person.

Like me, you may feel physically ill at the thought of going through this step. I understand, and that's why I've been praying for you as I have wrestled with each word, thought, and idea in this chapter. I invite you into my journey. It is my prayer that together, as we remove the false messages about forgiveness and rewrite our scripts with truth, we will become peacemakers. In the previous chapter we talked about breaking ties with generational sins and asking forgiveness from those whom we have hurt. In this chapter we'll focus on forgiving those who have hurt us. If ever there was a way to break ties with the sins committed against us, it is by choosing to forgive!

INITIATING PEACE WITH THOSE WHO HURT OR ANGERED US

Jesus said, "Blessed are the peacemakers, for they will be called sons of God" (Matthew 5:9). He wasn't encouraging us to live without conflict with others. This is impossible. As long as we live in a fallen world, there will be not only conflict but violence, abuse, and betrayal. The word *peacemaker* translates the Greek word *eireneuo*, which means "to bring to peace, to reconcile."[1] It speaks of taking action toward reconciliation. *Reconciliation* means "to change from enmity to friendship."[2] Peacemakers recognize that they can't *demand* reconciliation, they can only *initiate* it (see Romans 12:18). This is because several things must happen for reconciliation to occur. The offender needs to admit to wrongdoing, seek forgiveness, and then repent from the hurtful behavior. In addition, the person who has been hurt must be willing to forgive the offender. Reconciliation requires both forgiveness and repentance and is the decision of two.

But even if reconciliation is not possible, Jesus calls us to forgive! When Jesus hung dying from the cross, He prayed that the Father would forgive those crucifying Him (see Luke 23:34), but only those who came in repentance were reconciled (see Luke 13:3). If we do not come in repentance, we cannot be reconciled to God (see Acts 2:38; 17:30).

With that in mind we are going to use this definition for a peacemaker:

TO BE A PEACEMAKER MEANS:

to be a person who forgives.

PEACEMAKERS, NOT PEACEKEEPERS

Note that Jesus calls us to be *peacemakers*, not *peacekeepers*. This distinction is key. Peacekeepers keep peace at any and all costs. Their primary concern is avoiding conflict with other people for fear of creating friction. As a result, problematic issues are not resolved, and relationships are lived out on a surface level, with no one talking about what is really going on, or completely unravel. Jesus was a peacemaker, not a peacekeeper. He said, "Do not suppose that I have come to bring . . . peace, but a sword" (Matthew 10:34). The word for *peace* used here is not the same word that is used for *peacemaker*. This

Greek word means "harmonious relationships."[3] It carries the idea of an absence of conflict. Peacekeepers want everyone happy. Jesus understands not everyone is going to be happy, and that's okay. He did not come to bring an absence of conflict. He came to orchestrate reconciliation between God and people.

What Is the Difference Between a Peacekeeper and a Peacemaker?

Peacekeepers	Peacemakers
Don't rock the boat.	Make waves to create change.
Push issues under the carpet.	Bring issues to the surface.
Compromise boundaries.	Clarify boundaries.
Triangle (he said, she said).	Talk directly to people.
Demonstrate passive-aggressive behavior.	Express healthy anger.
Primary concern: avoiding conflict.	Primary concern: reconciliation.

A peacemaker, on the other hand, takes the initiative to restore the peace in a broken or strained relationship, *if it is safe to do so.*[4] Sometimes relationships are so toxic that it is best to no longer have any contact with the other person. Other times you may still have frequent contact, but the hurt lies underneath the surface of the relationship and presents itself in anger, fear, bitterness, or resentment.

While we can't control what the other person does, we can control what we do—we can control whether we forgive those who have hurt us. Even if reconciliation is not possible due to the other person's stubborn resistance or death, we have to forgive if we want to be obedient.

Still, God will never *make* us forgive. Only we can make that choice.

Let that sink in for a moment. It can be very empowering to realize you have a choice in this matter, particularly if the person you need to forgive hurt you when you were a defenseless child. But you aren't a child anymore, and you have the power to forgive those who hurt you. You can forgive or not forgive. The choice is completely yours.

One of the reasons many of us resist forgiveness, I believe, is because of the false ideas we have about forgiveness. So before I discuss practical steps for how to forgive, I want to help you identify misconceptions you may have about forgiveness so that you can correct them.

Rejecting False Messages About Forgiveness

One reason forgiveness was so hard for me was that I was so confused about what it was. By forgiving my abuser, was I saying that what he did was okay? Or that I would just sweep it under the carpet and pretend it never happened? Did it mean that I would forget the evil done to me?

My questions sent me on a quest to discover the truth about forgiveness. Here are some of the false messages I was able to identify:

1. Forgiveness means forgetting. I heard many times that I was supposed to "forgive and forget." In other words, forgiveness means wiping the event from my mind. I would read the following verse, which is talking about what God does when He forgives us, and wonder if it meant that He literally forgot: "For I will forgive their wickedness and will remember their sins no more" (Hebrews 8:12). As I studied this verse, I learned that many theologians agree that this doesn't mean God can't remember our sins anymore, because for Him to do this, His sovereignty would have to be compromised. Pastor and theologian R. T. Kendall wrote, "God doesn't literally forget our sins. He chooses to overlook them."[5] In other words, God chooses to not think about or dwell on our sins.

When we forgive, we can choose not to dwell on the harm done to us, but when someone has deeply hurt or harmed us, it's impossible to forget what happened. That's *not* how our minds work, except, perhaps, when a child experiences trauma so extreme that she cannot process what's happening to her. In such instances God allows the child's mind to block what happened from conscious memory. This is called dissociation. "A simple way to think about dissociation is to think of it as instant forgetting—amnesia, or a fractured mind. The brain has a switch that can deal with overwhelming feelings, and record them in a place that does not contact the conscious memory."[6] Though the person may not remember the trauma, he may exhibit symptoms of post-traumatic stress disorder.[7] A person who suffers from post-traumatic stress disorder suffers from amnesia following a traumatic event. Usually God allows the memory to resurface in His time.

2. Forgiveness excuses the sin. Another false message on our scripts is that if we forgive someone, it means we're saying, "What you did was okay." I used to think this. For years whenever people apologized to me I would tell them, "That's okay." It was as if I were exonerating them.

That's avoidance, not forgiveness.

If sins are excused rather than forgiven, unresolved issues continue to lie dormant, just under the surface. Given the right situation, those issues will rise to the surface again and at times feel more intense than before. Taryn's father called her stupid when she was a little girl and violently hit her for not being able to recite math facts quickly. Taryn never dealt with her anger. Instead, she made excuses for her father's behavior and avoided him. Years later, her son called her stupid in a fit of rage. Something in Taryn snapped. In anger she slapped her son several times across the face. Afterward, she felt horrible. She realized that because she had never forgiven her father, her anger lay dormant and resurfaced with her son.

Throughout the Gospels Jesus told people, "Your sins are forgiven."[8] He didn't mean that their wrong behavior was okay. It certainly was not okay; it was sin. When Jesus forgave, on occasion He told people to go and sin no more (see John 8:11).

3. Forgiveness means staying in a relationship with a person. Again, forgiveness is not the same as reconciliation. To be reconciled means that both parties are willing to do whatever is necessary for the relationship to be restored. You can forgive even if there cannot be reconciliation. When there's not been reconciliation, it might be wiser and more emotionally healthy for you to let go of the relationship.

Sometimes people misunderstand what the Bible means when it says to honor your parents (see Exodus 20:12). When parents have been abusive, it is difficult to find ways to honor them. As I have studied this verse, I have come to understand that to honor one's parents means to respect them in whatever way is possible. This may mean that you respect the fact that they gave you life and that you pray for them (even if they were abusive). Another way to honor parents is to recognize their good qualities while not forgetting the harm done to you and protecting yourself from further harm.

When someone hurts you, continues to hurt you, and shows no remorse, it can be harmful to stay in relationship with that person, no matter who that person is. In such instances being a peacemaker means forgiving that person while also adhering to strict boundaries that protect you from being hurt again. If the person you need to forgive can continue to hurt you, you may need to let the relationship go for God to do His deep inner work of healing in your life.

Just ask Geri. Her husband would, at times, fly into fits of rage. When he did, he hit her. Other times he attacked her verbally. Always, he would come back and apologize, and Geri always forgave him. Ultimately, even though Geri had forgiven her husband, she had to let go of the marriage because her safety and the safety of her children were at stake. She had to end the relationship because her husband did not change his abusive behavior.

4. Forgiveness pardons the offender from the consequences. Forgiveness is not pardoning the offender from the consequences of the sin that person committed. Forgiveness does not mean that you do not press charges against someone who has committed a crime against you or someone you love. A person still has to suffer the consequences for his sin, even if you forgive him.

Bridget told me that she had pressed charges against her neighbor for sexually assaulting her years earlier. He was convicted of the crime and now sits in jail as punishment. My friend has forgiven him and prays for him, but that did not mean that she shouldn't bring charges against him for the crime he had committed. He needed to experience the consequences of breaking the law, and other children needed to be protected from this predator.

If you have believed any of these false messages, you need to reject them and then replace them with the truth, which we'll explore next.

EMBRACING THE TRUTH ABOUT FORGIVENESS

The New Testament word for forgiveness, *aphiemi*, means "to send forth or away, let go from oneself. To let go from one's power, possession. To let go from one's further . . . attendance, occupancy."[9] Author Beth Moore has defined forgiveness as "our determined and deliberate willingness to let something go. To release it from our possession. To be willing and ready for it to no longer occupy us."[10]

In other words, when we forgive we let go.

We let go of our quest for revenge.

We let go of our anger.

We let go of our mental arguments.

We let go of our desire to punish.

We let go of our right for justice.

As I have been thinking, praying, and at times agonizing over what it means to forgive, I have identified four truths about forgiveness:

1. Forgiveness is a decision. If we wait till we feel like forgiving, we won't forgive. Instead, we must make a decision with our minds and trust God with our feelings of anger, fear, hurt, sorrow, betrayal, and so on. We can do this without denying or trying to hide those feelings. In fact, it's important to let God know how we feel so that we give the feelings to Him for safekeeping. He can handle our feelings much better than we can! Sometimes I literally say, "God, I give You my feelings of anger." I visualize myself handing all my anger over to Him. When I do this, I feel much more free from those feelings.

2. Forgiveness is a process. Our emotions are complicated. Often, it takes time to even recognize what we are feeling, so it might take some time to release those feelings to the Lord. It might happen incrementally. You might release some of your anger, only to learn a few months down the road that more anger needs to be released.

The Amish people living in Nickel Mines, Pennsylvania, understand that forgiveness is a process. On October 2, 2006, a gunman killed five innocent little girls in an Amish schoolhouse. The world has watched in astonishment as the Amish have forgiven. Steve Nolt, who coauthored *Amish Grace: How Forgiveness Transcended Tragedy*, said this about the Amish: "Their understanding of forgiveness is that it is a long process, that it is difficult, that it is painful, that replacing bitter feelings toward someone is something that takes time. . . . They begin with expressing their intention to forgive, with the faith that the emotional forgiveness will follow over months and years."[11] For the Nickel Mines Amish, the process began with their verbally expressing forgiveness and reaching out to the killer's family, embracing them as fellow victims. Do they ever experience waves of anger or sorrow now that they have forgiven? Sure. But they have taken the first step, trusting that their emotions will follow.

Here is an analogy that has helped me understand how forgiveness works as a process: When a person fractures a leg or an arm, sometimes there is so much swelling that doctors have to wait for the swelling to go down before setting the limb. The swelling in our broken hearts may need to diminish some before we can set them in the cast of forgiveness. One woman told me that it took her only one day after she found out that her husband had had an affair to forgive him. I doubt that she had truly forgiven him for a hurt that deep. Forgiveness takes time. Her feelings had to settle a bit before she would be able to forgive.

3. Forgiveness is often excruciating. I wish I could tell you that forgiveness is easy. It's just not. Our self-protective instincts are too strong. We want to take revenge. We desire to "get even." We may even wish we could destroy the offender's credibility or image. These feelings are normal; even after we've decided to forgive, some of these feelings may resurface. We may be making great progress in our forgiveness journey and out of the blue find ourselves once again feeling angry or sad. This is normal and how the forgiveness process works.

The Holy Spirit does strengthen us, but even then forgiveness can still feel excruciating. The offense might still cause hurt. The choice to forgive doesn't erase the pain of the hurt, but it does ease the pain. This choice is sometimes the most difficult part of the journey. Emotional release may not follow right away.

Paul wrote, "I have been crucified with Christ and I no longer live, but Christ lives in me" (Galatians 2:20). Every time we make the choice to forgive, we have an opportunity to join Christ in His crucifixion. We are invited into "the fellowship of . . . his suffering" (Philippians 3:10). The word *excruciating* comes from the word *crucify*.[12] It was excruciating for Jesus to be crucified, which was necessary for Him to forgive us. When someone tells me that forgiveness is easy, I have to wonder if they have forgotten what it took for God to forgive us!

4. Forgiveness benefits you, not your offender. We are the ones who benefit when we choose to forgive. Author Jane Rubietta wrote, "Nothing I do to punish another for hurting me brings me healing."[13] Healing comes when we let go. If we hold on, we build up bitterness in our hearts.

Bitterness is the monument we build to our pain. It says we don't want to forgive, we are angry, and we want the other person to "pay" for the hurt done to us. When we rehearse our hurt, we create monuments of bitterness. Those monuments of bitterness build a protective wall around our hearts. The problem is that the wall we construct to protect our hearts can be the same wall that shuts out the Holy Spirit's voice in our lives. Susan Lee, a dancer who was brutally raped, vividly describes the effect of bitterness on the soul: "It is as stifling as a muffled scream, a voiceless cry. It is an awesome feeling of helplessness and hurt, a trapped feeling worse than death itself."[14] Of course, Susan felt violated, angry, bitter, and frightened at first. But as she considered the alternative to living with bitterness, she chose forgiveness.

Recently, I spoke at a women's retreat. One of the messages I gave was on forgiveness. Maria began to weep after I finished speaking. She moaned, "I can't, I can't!" All of a sudden she ran out of the room and vomited. When she reentered she said, "I realize now that my bitterness is making me literally sick. If I choose to forgive I am letting bitterness go." Another woman wrote that she had suffered intense back pain for years. After hearing the message on forgiveness, she went to the foot of the cross and released her anger, hurt, and bitterness over an event that had happened fifteen years earlier. After agreeing with God to forgive, she stood up, pain-free for the first time in years. She wrote that since that time, she has not had any more back pain.

You see, forgiveness sets us free. I know. When I chose to forgive my abuser, he no longer held me captive. Before I forgave him, I saw him as very powerful because of the prominent position he held. After I forgave him, I realized he wasn't so big. I allowed myself to consider what would make a man grow up to abuse children. This made me feel sorry for him rather than hate him. I realized that the power he possessed had distorted his thinking. He was tangled in his own stuff. Did he ever repent? Not that I know of, but that is in God's hands. I like the way Philip Yancey said it: "Forgiveness is an act of faith. By forgiving another, I am trusting that God is a better justice-maker than I am. By forgiving, I release my own right to get even and leave all issues of fairness for God to work out. I leave in God's hands the scales that must balance justice and mercy."[15]

Oh, my friend, I don't know what your hurt is. Perhaps it is horrific. Will you dare to begin the journey of forgiveness?

But . . . How?

Forgiveness is a challenging and frightening hike. It doesn't happen in neat steps. Sometimes the path is arduous and terribly messy. Having said that, here are steps I took that moved me further on my journey toward forgiveness. These steps might look different in your life. You might need to take some but not all of them. As you read each step, seek God. Ask Him if this is a step that would be helpful to you.

We've already talked about the first step, which is making the decision to forgive. Now let's take a look at the next steps:

Break the Silence

Once I'd made the decision to forgive, I needed to admit just how much sexual abuse had damaged my emotional script. The old messages of "don't tell, don't feel" were holding me captive. I had to break the code of silence, admit what had happened, and face how badly it hurt.

The first person I did this with was a godly, state-licensed counselor. She said something I will never forget: "Sin multiplies in silence." I also told my godly, mature mentor. And, as you read at the beginning of this chapter, I also told a Christian leader. Staying silent was like staying stuck. I couldn't forgive without admitting the extent of the pain and asking for help from others.

It is the only path to healing. Kathy Olsen, author of *Silent Pain*, agrees. She wrote, "This very silence, this reluctance to face the pain, separates us from the vital parts of our souls that have been damaged."[16] I found this to be true in my life. If I refused to talk and process the horrible things that happened to me, the emotions associated with those horrors became stuck inside of me. Before I started talking about the abuse, I couldn't find my feelings. (I have since found out that this is very normal for those who have been abused.) As a result, I felt numb, almost as if there were a part of me that was dead. It was as if I had built protective walls around my soul, distancing myself from the hurt and pain. I had to tear down those walls and look at what had happened to me; I had to look pain in the face. I couldn't run from it anymore. I couldn't pretend it wasn't so bad anymore. I had to face the amount of damage it had done to my soul. And I had to talk. Talking helped me find those feelings and get them out.

While this step is very important, it can be excruciating and costly.

Because I broke the code of silence and brought the truth to light, I lost several key relationships. I cannot express how difficult this has been, but I also know that until I admitted the depth of my hurt, I could not forgive.

Express Your Anger

For years I had no idea how angry I was about what had happened to me. Then one day I was reading a book about a girl who had been abused, and I became so agitated I threw the book across the room and fell on the floor sobbing. When that happened, I knew I had to do something about my anger. Oh, this was very hard for me. I told you in chapter 3 that I grew up believing anger was wrong. I was mistaken. Anger is not wrong. It is a natural emotion experienced when we or others we love are hurt or treated unfairly. But what we do with our anger can be wrong, which is why we need to express it in healthy ways (see the sidebar on page 175). In time, I realized I had to express my anger in order to move toward forgiveness, and I began to write down my angry feelings in a journal.

Remember the Old Testament story of Joseph? I believe his story illustrates that expressing our anger is often a part of the forgiveness process. Joseph could be the poster child for dysfunctional families. In case you've forgotten, he was "Daddy's favorite." There's always a high price for being Daddy's favorite! Joseph's brothers got sick of the special perks he was receiving and decided to get rid of him. Wanting to make a few bucks, they sold him into slavery, but they told their father that Joseph had been killed by a wild animal. From that point on, there is a huge, dark family secret. That secret ruled the family. No family vacations down to Egypt to visit the pyramids because no one wants Dad to find out the truth.

But years later a famine changed all that, and Joseph's brothers were forced to go to Egypt to buy food. Guess who was in charge of the food supply? Joseph. They didn't recognize him, but he recognized them and expressed his anger toward them. How did he do that? He spoke harshly to them (see Genesis 42:7), accused them of being spies (see Genesis 42:9), tested them, putting one of his brothers in jail (see Genesis 42:24), and played a few mind games with them (see Genesis 42:25). I don't know about you, but these sound like expressions of anger to me.

Did he express his anger correctly? None of us can know his heart, but it sure looks as if Joseph wanted his brothers to sweat a little, which would be a very human response. (Despite Joseph's godly character, he wasn't perfect!) However, after he expressed his anger, he came clean with his brothers and confronted them with what they did: "I am your brother Joseph, the one you sold into Egypt!" (Genesis 45:4). Confrontation is often an important part of the forgiveness process.

HEALTHY VERSUS UNHEALTHY EXPRESSIONS OF ANGER

Healthy	Unhealthy
Using "I" statements— "I feel angry"	Emotional blackmail
Speaking firmly—even using a harsh tone	Screaming or yelling
Being assertive	Being aggressive
Seeking justice	Retaliation
Journaling your feelings	Stuffing your feelings
Discussing feelings	Silent smoldering
Physical exertion	Becoming violent

Consider Confronting

Most of us don't like confrontation, particularly if we were raised with the philosophy of "peace at any and all costs." However, the Bible tells us:

> Confront people directly. (Leviticus 19:17, NLT)
> If your brother sins against you, go and show him his fault. (Matthew 18:15)

The purpose for a confrontation is to "face someone with the facts as we see them and to open up dialogue."[17] Confrontation gives voice to the hurt we have experienced and allows us to hear our offender's perspective. However, if the offense is violent, as in sexual or physical abuse, rape, or murder, then we don't need to listen to our perpetrator's perspective; we need to hear repentance. In a confrontation we focus on the offense, not the offender. We are assertive, but not aggressive. We don't attack the person. We don't confront to punish or embarrass.

So before you confront, *examine your motives*. Biblically, I see three reasons to confront:

1. To repair a broken relationship (see Matthew 5:23-25; 18:15-18). For example, a friend breaks your confidence. Instead of ending the friendship or quietly withdrawing, confront her with the offense so that it can be brought out in the open. Confrontation gives the offender the opportunity to seek forgiveness and to make amends, if necessary. The goal for confronting is reconciliation.

CONFRONTATION

The Purpose: to open dialogue
The Focus: the problem
The Goal: reconciliation

Sandra's relationship with her father was estranged due to his sexual abuse. After several years of counseling, she decided to take a bold step. In the presence of her therapist, she confronted her father, telling him the pain the abuse had caused her over the years. Weeping, Sandra's father got on his knee and asked his daughter to forgive him. Sandra was reconciled to her father before his death, in part because she found the courage to confront him.

2. To restore a sense of dignity (see Genesis 1:27; Matthew 18:15-18). Each of us was created with a God-given sense of dignity, because we were created in the image of God. Some sins committed against us violate our dignity. When we confront, we have an opportunity to rewrite our emotional scripts by restoring our dignity.

My abuser was dead before I began dealing with my memories of sexual abuse. Because of this, I could not confront him face-to-face. So instead, I confronted him through a letter. Obviously, he didn't read the letter, but that letter allowed me to verbalize my anger and how the abuse had impacted my life. In that letter I told him that the abuse made me feel as though I had no value or worth, which is a lie. God created me with intrinsic value and worth. By writing that letter, I restored my sense of dignity.

3. To reestablish justice (Proverbs 8:9). Children cannot speak out for themselves. They need an advocate to reestablish justice for them. When one of our children was in the first grade, she asked to use the restroom during lunch. The lunch monitor told her no and swore at her, using some very inappropriate language. Steve and I were furious. He went to the school and confronted the lunch monitor and reported her to the principal. He reestablished justice for our six-year-old, who was not able to do the confronting herself.

After you've examined your motives, ***plan out what you will say.*** Confrontations can be emotional, and it's easy to get pulled into a destructive verbal exchange. Release any and all expectations to the Lord. Remind yourself that the purpose of your confrontation is not to convince the other person of your correctness. This is important, because the confrontation may not be received well—at least at first. For example, you might want to say, "When you *(state the offense)* it made me feel _____. It affected my *(state the areas of your life that it affected: your self-esteem, views of sexuality, view of God, and so on)."*

If possible, meet in person. If the person poses a physical threat to you, take someone or several people with you. If the offender poses an emotional threat to you or if the person is dead, craft a letter. E-mails are generally not a good way to go because it is too easy to hit the send key without prayerfully considering the ramifications. Trust me, I've learned the hard way!

After you have given voice to your feelings, listen. Allow your offender to speak, but ask the Lord to guard your heart and mouth. Your offender might try to pull you into a debate. Listen, but don't enter into an emotional battle. This is extremely difficult, but emotionally charged debates are usually counterproductive.

In a confrontation the best-case scenario would be if the offender apologizes and reconciliation takes place. However, sometimes confrontations are met with denial. The person may refuse to acknowledge any wrongdoing. He or she may lash out in anger. Either way, Jesus invites us to "let go" and move forward.

Let go of your mental arguments, trying to prove you are right.

Let go of your desire to see the other person's reputation ruined.

Let go of your desire to "get even" or punish the other person.

Verbalize Your Forgiveness to God

Notice that I did not say verbalize your forgiveness to your offender. Unless that person asks for your forgiveness, it is usually not a good idea to verbalize forgiveness because your offender may tell you that he or she didn't do anything wrong. Then you might be tempted to argue with the person, and this is counterproductive to forgiveness. Instead, verbalize your forgiveness to God; this makes it more concrete in your mind.

This was the step I had missed before talking with the Christian leader. It wasn't enough for me to decide in my mind that I wanted to forgive. I needed to tell God, "I forgive him." Like the Amish, I realized that when you verbalize your forgiveness, it is an act of faith. You state you will forgive and you trust that your feelings and emotions will follow.

I believe Joseph verbalized forgiveness when he told his brothers, "And now, do not be distressed and do not be angry with yourselves for selling me here" (Genesis 45:5). His statement shows us that he had let go of any bitterness, any desire for revenge, any anger, and any desire to punish. In fact, he went on to say, "Because it was to save lives that God sent me ahead."

Move Beyond the Role of a Victim

One way we move forward is by no longer thinking of ourselves as victims. Every time a victim mentality sets in, remind yourself that you have forgiven. You are no longer held captive by your perpetrator. He or she no longer has any hold on you.

Joseph moved beyond the role of a victim when he told his brothers, "You intended to harm me, but God intended it for good to accomplish what is now being done, the saving of many lives" (Genesis 50:20). You can move beyond the role of a victim by realizing that the same is true about the evil done to you. God can use it for good. Even if there has not been reconciliation, God can use your story to help others, as He is using mine.

When we understand this, it helps us move beyond the pain so that we can see the beauty that can come out of horror. Choose some area of your personal life in which to grow. Learn a new skill. Reach out to someone in your community. Meditate on who you are in Christ. In other words, move beyond the role of a victim; you are more than your hurts.

If your spouse is the one you needed to make peace with, invite him to take up a new hobby with you, such as in-line skating, motorbiking, painting, or photography. Or take a vacation somewhere. By these actions, you are symbolizing that the old offense is gone and your relationship has been made new.

Celebrate Closure

Once you have admitted the truth, expressed your anger, considered confronting, verbalized your forgiveness, and moved beyond the role of a victim, celebrate closure. Even if there are many layers in your forgiveness process, celebrate the closure of each layer. After I released all the memories to the Lord and told Him I was willing to forgive, I wrote about it in my journal. I can always look back and find that dated entry and remind myself that I have forgiven my abuser. I also treated myself to a Starbucks. (Okay, maybe I could have thought of a more profound way to celebrate . . . but I like coffee.) When we celebrate closure, it gives us a sense of accomplishment and freedom. While God may reveal more that you need to forgive, you have successfully dealt with one layer. Each layer can mean a new celebration.

Pray for Your Enemy to Be Blessed

One step remains: Pray for God's blessing in the life of your offender. Jesus said, "Love your enemies and pray for those who persecute you" (Matthew 5:44). When we are willing to pray for our enemies to be blessed and forgiven, our emotional scripts are transformed and we become more like Christ than ever before. As a result, we experience deeper peace than we ever imagined.

In chapter 3 we talked about Job. When God allowed Job to be tested by Satan, Job's friends did not support or comfort him. Instead, they criticized him. At the end of the story those friends came to Job and he prayed for them. The Bible then tells us, "After Job had prayed for his friends, the LORD made him prosperous" (Job 42:10). In other words, God was pleased with Job's response. He was pleased that although Job's friends had hurt him, Job found the courage to forgive them and to pray for them. What a powerful example of how choosing to pray for your enemies brings blessing from God. While God does not always choose to bless us financially, He blesses us with a peace that goes beyond human understanding. This is what He did in my life.

AT PEACE

At the beginning of this book I told you how I never wanted sexual abuse to be a part of my story. I can't change what happened to me, but I can change how I respond. I can rewrite the script. Now my script reads "peacemaker." By forgiving my abuser, I have made peace with the sexual abuse of my past. The memories no longer haunt me. While

I could not be reconciled to my abuser because I had no memories of the abuse until after he had died, I have forgiven him and become reconciled to my story. What about you? Are you ready to embark on the journey of forgiveness so that you too can be at peace? If so, erase the false messages that you have believed about forgiveness, embrace the truth about forgiveness, and begin by making at least one of the choices that I made — *verbalize to God your willingness to forgive.*

PRAYING SCRIPTURE
TO INTERNALIZE TRUTH

Father God, my heart cries out with the psalmist, "Praise the Lord, O my soul; all my inmost being, praise his holy name. Praise the Lord, O my soul, and forget not all his benefits—who forgives all your sins and heals all your diseases, who redeems your life from the pit and crowns you with love and compassion" (Psalm 103:1-4). Thank you for Your grace in my life. Thank you that when I was still a sinner You died for me (see Romans 5:8). I praise You that I am now reconciled to God the Father through Your finished work on the cross (see Romans 5:11).

Holy One, Your Word tells me that if I forgive others when they sin against me, my Father in heaven will also forgive me. It also tells me that if I do not forgive others their sins, You will not forgive my sins (see Matthew 6:14-15). Lord, this verse is hard to understand, and sometimes I am tempted to rationalize. But You repeat the same concept in Luke 6:37, "Forgive, and you will be forgiven." God, You tell me You are not interested in my gifts if I have not forgiven my brother (see Matthew 5:23-24). When Peter asked how many times he needed to forgive, You told him seventy-seven times (see Matthew 18:21-22). Lord, that's a lot of times to offer forgiveness. In the parable of the unmerciful steward (see Matthew 18:23-35) the price of not forgiving was monumental. Help me to see how important it is to You that I forgive. God, my flesh is so reluctant to offer forgiveness; help me to understand the repercussions of not forgiving. Holy Spirit, bring my will into alignment with the Father's. Give me the heart of Jesus, I pray.

Your Word warns me not to let any bitter root grow in my heart (see Hebrews 12:15). Your Word also warns me not to let Satan outwit me (see 2 Corinthians 2:11). If I refuse to forgive, Satan wins and I live in bondage to my offender. Help me to remember that I triumph every time I choose to forgive, because mercy triumphs over judgment (see James 2:12-13). Thank you that every time I forgive, I can overcome evil with good (see Romans 12:21).

Lord, You tell me that when others treat me in an evil manner, I am not to repay evil with evil or insult with insult, but with blessings, because I am Your child (see 1 Peter 3:9). Help me to remember that You are in Your holy temple (see Habakkuk 2:20), and that I can trust You with justice. You promise me that You will repay me for the years the locusts have eaten (see Joel 2:25). So I will choose to wait for You, Lord. You will deliver me in Your time (see Proverbs 20:22).

FURTHER TRANSFORMATION
Digging Deeper into the Scriptures

1. Meditate on and memorize 1 Peter 3:9 as written here or in another translation.

   Do not repay evil with evil or insult with insult, but with blessing, because to this you were called so that you may inherit a blessing.

2. Read Matthew 5:23-24 and 6:14. Why do you think Jesus places such high value on forgiving others?

3. Read Genesis 37 (the story of Joseph being thrown into a pit and sold by his brothers). Make a list of the messages that you think were written on Joseph's emotional script.

4. How do you think choosing to forgive helped rewrite Joseph's emotional script?

5. Read Matthew 18:21-35. This passage teaches the parable of the unmerciful servant. Why do you think Jesus taught this parable? What does this parable teach about the importance of forgiveness?

6. When you hear the word *confront*, what comes to your mind? Read Matthew 18:15-20. Based on this passage, do you think Jesus thought confrontations were a good thing or a bad thing? What principles are given in this passage about how and when confrontations should happen?

7. Read 2 Corinthians 5:18-19. In your own words, write a job description for a minister of reconciliation.

Probing Deeper into Your Emotional Script

8. Read through the false messages about forgiveness on pages 166-169. Have you believed any of those false messages about forgiveness? If so, which one(s)? What messages were written on your emotional script about forgiveness? How did reading that section help clear up any misunderstandings you might have had about forgiveness?

9. Would you describe yourself as a peacekeeper or a peacemaker? What messages were written on your emotional script about peacekeeping? What lessons did you learn in this chapter about becoming a peacemaker?

10. Read back over the steps of forgiveness outlined under the section titled "But . . . How?" (see pages 172-180). Think of someone you need to forgive. Which of these steps is the most challenging for you personally? Why? What has God spoken to you through this chapter?

11. One of the truths taught in this chapter is that forgiving benefits you, not your offender. How could forgiving your enemies benefit you personally?

12. Unleash the power of praise. Read and meditate on Psalm 103. Choose several verses of this psalm and write a paraphrase of them, praising God for His goodness in your life.

CHAPTER 9

REWRITE YOUR DEFINITION OF JOY

Blessed are those who are persecuted because of righteousness,
for theirs is the kingdom of heaven.
Blessed are you when people insult you,
persecute you and falsely say all kinds of evil against you
because of me.
Rejoice and be glad, because great is your reward in heaven.

MATTHEW 5:10-12

Molly had made huge progress on rewriting her emotional script. A committed team composed of a licensed counselor, a godly mentor, and a pastor had come alongside her during a crisis in her marriage that precipitated her willingness to begin rewriting her script. Molly had become desperate and determined, she had grieved her losses, she had put on meekness and given up control, she had set her appetite on God, extended mercy, uprooted generational sin, and even forgiven her husband for an affair and for lashing out at her in anger. God had taken an emotional script that read "peace at any cost" and had begun rewriting it to read "strong and courageous."

During the process of rewriting her script, the Lord used a verse in 1 Peter to strengthen Molly: "Live as free men, but do not use your freedom as a cover-up for evil" (2:16). Molly realized her passivity about her husband's violent outbursts had become a cover-up for evil, so she began to take a stand, calling the police and reporting Mark's violent behavior. The only problem? Mark, Molly's husband, didn't appreciate the new script.

Mark wanted his old wife back—the one who would not take a stand against his abuse of alcohol. The one who would cower when he flew into fits of rage and the one who would keep allowing him to come home, even after sexual flings. Instead, the new Molly was strong enough to report Mark and obtain a restraining order. The more Molly took a stand for righteousness, the more Mark's threats increased. Finally, for her own safety and the safety of her children, she had to take the ultimate stand and leave. Mark responded with divorce papers, complaining that Molly had become too religious. As a Christ follower she felt grieved that she had to sign the divorce papers, but Mark left her no other option.

Persecution forced Molly to figure out her most important value. It could no longer be "peace at any cost" and the approval of others. Instead, it had to be the approval of Christ. Molly's joy had to be found purely in Christ. Recently, she wrote to me and described the intimacy she has since discovered in Christ. When asked whether the rewriting was worth it, Molly answered categorically, "Yes!" The new joy she has discovered in Christ has been worth all the pain she experienced to get there.

Jesus said, "Blessed are those who are persecuted because of righteousness, for theirs is the kingdom of heaven. Blessed are you when people insult you, persecute you and falsely say all kinds of evil against you because of me. Rejoice and be glad" (Matthew 5:10-12). Notice that Jesus didn't say, "*If* people insult you, persecute you, and falsely say all kinds of evil against you." He said, "*When* people insult you, persecute you, and falsely say all kinds of evil against you."

I love the way author Dorothy Kelley Patterson has said it: "For you to follow Christ, to think His thoughts, and to adopt His ways will put you under condemnation by those who are in opposition to Him."[1] In other words, if you rewrite your emotional script and become like Christ, you *will* take heat for your choices. You might not be killed for your faith, but you *will* experience hostility.

As I have been thinking about this, I have come to realize that when you take steps to become more like Christ and more emotionally healthy, it impacts your relationships. Some won't like the changes and so you will experience kickback. The kickback is the plea of those close to you who want you to return to the old you. For example, you might not have set healthy boundaries in the past, and now you are comfortable setting those boundaries. As a result, you are not so easily manipulated. People who are used to manipulating you are not going to like this, and they will push back. Others may not like it that you have given up old pleasures. Since you have set your appetite on God and His righteousness, those old pleasures don't hold the same lure. Or perhaps you don't fit as well with your family since you have uprooted the generational sins. Don't become discouraged. Instead, recognize that according to Jesus, what you are experiencing is normal.

TRANSFORMATION CAN BRING PERSECUTION

Let's take a closer look at what Jesus said: "Blessed are you when people insult you, persecute you and falsely say all kinds of evil against you" (Matthew 5:11). It's almost as if He was afraid we'd misunderstand what He meant by *persecution*, so He listed three ways we can be persecuted:

1. Verbal Insults: "When People Insult You"

Verbal insults carry the idea of taunting and abusive words. When you start changing as a result of rewriting your script, others will notice. Some of the people closest to you may not like it because your choices impact them. They may not be ready to do the rewriting that you have done. As a result, they become uncomfortable and may lash out with verbal insults.

For example: One husband witnessing the changes in his wife said, "I don't like the changes you have made. I can't control you anymore." A friend of mine told me that her mother complained to her, "All my friends say that you are disrespectful. They are wondering what's happened to you. You're not very nice anymore. We used to be so close." All because she set healthy boundaries.

Sometimes the Evil One himself taunts us. He lives to accuse us (see Revelation 12:10). As soon as you attempt to rewrite your emotional script, you can count on his snide accusations. As soon as I began telling my story and speaking on the topic of forgiveness, Satan began to taunt me with messages of guilt: "You shouldn't let the secret out." He attacked me with messages of shame: "How can God use such a messy story?" He attacked me with insults: "You shouldn't speak; you cannot communicate well!" He attacked me with messages of discouragement: "Just quit. No life change is happening in the women to whom you speak." Many times right before I get up to speak, particularly on the topic of forgiveness, I suddenly forget my outline, have choking sensations, experience great anxiety, and begin to think, *What am I doing up here? I want to go home. I can't do this.* Satan does not want God's message of forgiveness and freedom to reach women. Sometimes his attacks come not only before I speak but after. I second-guess everything I've just taught or I sink down into depression. When Satan hurls insults at me, I have learned to fill my mind with Scriptures such as Revelation 12:11: "They overcame him [the accuser] by the blood of the Lamb and by the word of their testimony." I have also learned the importance of having prayer warriors uphold me before and after I speak.

Please understand, I don't say all that to frighten you. I tell you this to make you aware. Satan is our enemy. He "prowls around like a roaring lion looking for someone to devour" (1 Peter 5:8). Learn to use your sword, the Word of God, so that you won't be overcome by the accuser.

2. Harassment and Other Forms of Persecution: "Persecute You"

The Greek word used here for *persecute* means pursuing, harassing, troubling. It creates a picture of "the world running after or pursuing believers in order to cause them suffering."[2] Persecution can involve physical assaults, but it can also involve legal action. For example, as you read in the opening story of this chapter, Molly's husband pursued her and eventually took legal action against her, all because she rewrote her emotional script.

I know parents who have cut their kids out of the will because of the rewriting their children have done. One husband took legal action against his wife after she rewrote her emotional script, telling lawyers that she was "emotionally unfit" to have custody of their children. Each of these is an example of the type of harassment Jesus spoke about.

3. Defamation of Character: "Falsely Say All Kinds of Evil Against You"

Unfortunately, sometimes this type of persecution comes even from within the church. Satan will often use the mouths of believers to defame the life of another follower of Christ, even believers who have rewritten their emotional scripts and have chosen to become emotionally healthy. Sometimes this type of persecution comes in the form of gossip. One friend complained about another friend, "She's not any fun anymore. She's become too holy or something."

Though difficult to endure, each of these types of persecution—verbal insults, harassment, or defamation of character—can be used by God to further rewrite our scripts. One way God uses all three is to rewrite our definition of joy.

ALLOWING PERSECUTION TO REWRITE OUR DEFINITION OF JOY

We have all grown up understanding that joy means feelings of happiness that are experienced when life is going well. That's what is written on our emotional scripts. Even the dictionary defines *joy* as "the emotion of great delight or happiness caused by something exceptionally good or satisfying: keen pleasure; elation."[3] Based on our old scripts, when life goes well, joy seems attainable. But when life takes a turn for the worse, joy feels elusive. Part of the role that persecution plays is clarifying that definition of joy. Let me explain.

I decided to do a little research on how joy develops and came across this:

> We now know that a "joy center" exists in the right orbital prefrontal cortex of the brain. It has executive control over the entire emotional system. When the joy center has been sufficiently developed, it regulates emotions, pain control and immunity centers; it guides us to act like ourselves; it releases neurotransmitters like dopamine and serotonin; and it is the only part of the brain that overrides the main drive centers—food and sexual impulses, terror and rage.[4]

This joy center develops in infancy. Neurologists and psychologists now say "that the basic human need is to be the 'sparkle in someone's eye.'"[5]

When infants see joy in the eyes of their parents, the joy center of their brain is developed. If the joy center develops correctly, an individual can find the path back to joy, in spite of the most difficult traumas. Because we live in a fallen world, most of us will experience trauma of some kind. The exciting thing is that even if your joy center did not develop properly, it can be repaired and restored. Research has now proved that this is one of three parts of the brain that can regenerate.[6]

This is where our relationships with God become critical. When we receive Him as Savior, we also receive Him as Abba Father, and we become the sparkle of His eye. The more we live in intimate fellowship with Him, the more we recognize the look of love in His eyes and the more our joy center develops. The more intimate our relationships with

God, then, the deeper our joy.

I define joy like this:

> *Joy is deeply rooted peace and happiness*
> *that is based on the knowledge that*
> *I am the sparkle in Abba's eye.*

My husband, Steve, has also rewritten his definition of joy. Persecution prompted the rewriting. In one of the churches where we served, a certain group of influential people did not like the direction Steve was taking the church, so they started rumors defaming his character. The pressure was so great on Steve that he felt he needed to resign.

After doing so, he fell into a time of deep introspection and began to realize the truth about what was written on his emotional script. He discovered that his emotional script led him to define joy as "feeling successful." He had entered the ministry when he was young, and he climbed the ministry ladder of success. His identity was wrapped up in being a senior pastor. When everything fell apart, he was forced into solitude, where the Holy Spirit helped him rewrite his script.

I watched as my husband became more compassionate, more content, more concerned with his relationship with Christ than with how successful he was. As I write this, we are just now reentering the pastorate. Steve has changed. His identity is rooted in Christ and his joy and ministry are the overflow of his intimate walk with God. Persecution has knit his soul together with Christ. They have become kindred spirits in suffering.

If you are walking through a time of persecution, God can use it to help you to further rewrite your script. He may be allowing the heat to help you redefine your definition of joy. Joy at this moment may feel unattainable. Let's take a look at how you can build your joy center so that no matter what persecution you might be facing you can experience joy.

STRENGTHENING YOUR JOY CENTER

The apostle Paul is a great example of someone who rejoiced even in the midst of hardship and persecution. He knew he was treasured and deeply loved by Abba Father. This allowed him to rejoice no matter what the circumstances he was facing. He wrote a letter to the church in Philippi while sitting in a jail cell. That letter provides some of the greatest secrets for how to rejoice, even under fire. In some ways, we could look at them as ways to strengthen our joy centers.

While the number thirteen is usually considered unlucky, it is different in the book of Philippians. The thirteenth verse of each chapter offers us four life-changing secrets for strengthening our joy centers. Let's take a look at those verses.

Look for the Blessing

Paul wrote, "As a result, it has become clear throughout the whole palace guard and to everyone else that I am in chains for Christ" (1:13). Paul was in prison for sharing his faith. His circumstances stank. I doubt he was the sparkle in the guards' eyes. Paul was under house arrest in Rome, which meant he had guards chained to him 24/7. He had a *captive* audience to hear the gospel of Jesus Christ; they certainly weren't going anywhere. Paul rejoiced because of his amazing opportunity! (If Paul was in prison in Rome, as most Bible commentators believe, then that means nine thousand prison guards heard the gospel, as there were generally that many in the palace guard. That's a lot of people who heard the gospel.)

In every dark circumstance, we can find a blessing. When we look for the blessing, we cultivate an attitude of gratitude, which results in joy, which strengthens our joy centers. I have a friend who is very good at finding the blessing in all of life's dark circumstances. Jill will be telling me about her husband's cancer, and then she'll say, "But the blessing is we've discovered how much our friends love us." Or "But the blessing is that we had the opportunity to share Christ with the doctor." Jill is always searching for the blessing in each challenge. She doesn't deny the pain or difficulty that their family is going through. She embraces the reality of her circumstances, but at the same time, she trusts in God's sovereignty and knows that good can come out of evil. Jill keeps a blessing journal in which she records one blessing every day. Jill is taking an active step to build up her joy center.

Recognize God Is at Work in You

Paul wrote, "For it is God who works in you to will and to act according to his good purpose" (Philippians 2:13). No matter how grim your circumstances, if you have the indwelling Christ, then God is at work in your life. He might be teaching you to trust Him more, He might be taking you deeper into experiencing His love, or He might be weaving courage into your life. He uses every difficult circumstance to shape and mold you into the image of His Son, Jesus Christ.

When your life feels dark, take a few moments and analyze, "How is God at work in my life?" If you make a list of all the ways you see Him at work in your life, you will feel amazed, and you will strengthen your joy center.

When I walked through the dark valley of breast cancer, I felt depressed at times, and so I began to ask myself, "How is God at work in my life, using cancer as the tool?" I realized that He used breast cancer to make some significant revisions in my emotional script. I had lots of time to do nothing but rest and realized during that time that I didn't need to always perform for God. He also helped me see that my body was His sanctuary, and that as His sanctuary it was beautiful with or without breasts. He allowed me to find greater joy in the simple things of life—such as taking a walk, enjoying a conversation with my children, or simply savoring a beautiful day. He gave me new boldness and many opportunities to share how my faith had brought me hope during breast cancer. As a result, I became a much calmer person. When I recognized how deeply God was working in my life, I experienced joy.

Forsake the Old Script, Focus on the New Script

Paul wrote, "Brothers, I do not consider myself yet to have taken hold of it. But one thing I do: Forgetting what is behind and straining toward what is ahead" (3:13). Paul is creating a picture here of a runner running a race. The runner may be making great time. But if he looks back, he will lose speed, direction, and eventually the race itself. The same holds true when it comes to rewriting your emotional script.

When persecution comes, if you look back and start rehearsing the old messages of your script instead of remembering the sparkle in the Father's eye, you will despair. It's not enough to try to forget and push those messages from your mind. Instead, you must *forsake* the messages written on your old script and fill your mind with God's messages for your new script. Remind yourself that:

- You are treasured and valued by the Father (see Isaiah 43:4).
- You are engraved on the palms of His hands. He will not abandon you (see Isaiah 49:15-16).
- You are holy and deeply loved (Colossians 3:12).
- You are His unique poem, created for His pleasure (Ephesians 2:10).

As you rehearse God's messages to you, you'll remember the sparkle in His eye. It will help you return to joy and gladness.

Remember the Promised Power Available to You

Finally, Paul wrote, "I can do everything through him who gives me strength" (4:13). When Jesus spoke to His disciples, preparing them for His departure and the persecution they would face for His sake, He said, "It is for your good that I am going away. Unless I go away, the Counselor will not come to you; but if I go, I will send him to you" (John 16:7).

When we come to an understanding of the indwelling Christ, it infuses us with holy confidence. Anything He calls us to do we can do because His power flows through us. He speaks gently to us, saying, "Do not fear the reproach of men or be terrified by their insults" (Isaiah 51:7).

Growing up, I heard many sermons about people being persecuted in other parts of the world. The thought of being persecuted terrified me. I can remember praying, *What if I'm not strong enough to stand up and say, "I love You," Jesus?* That fear haunted me for years, probably into adult life. I haven't faced much persecution, but as I mentioned earlier, I have faced some heat for rewriting my script and talking about the sexual abuse I experienced as a child. This has been difficult for me, so I've continued to seek the Lord, asking Him, *Should I continue to share my story?* His answer is always the same: "Becky, give me your mouth. I am calling you to bring hope to hurting women." I have had to continually look at the loving gaze of my Abba. When I look at the sparkle in His eye, I am able to do what He has called me to do with less fear and more joy. I have learned to cling, not just loosely but tightly, desperately, vehemently cling, to the promises in the Word for those who face the fire.

So what are those promises?

His grace will provide what you need in the moment. God's grace is *always* sufficient, no matter our lives' circumstances (see 2 Corinthians 12:9). Jesus promised His disciples that when they faced dignitaries and others who would put them on trial, they were not to worry because the indwelling spirit of Christ would give them the words they would need (see Matthew 10:19). He will do the same for you. You will *never* face any situation without His grace. You will *never* need more grace than He provides. It will be enough!

In 1555 when Thomas Hauker was sitting in a jail cell in England, knowing that the next day he would be burned at the stake, his cellmate whispered, "Thomas, I have to know. I need to know if what the others say about the grace of God is true. Tomorrow, when they burn you at the stake, if the pain is tolerable and your mind is still at peace, lift your hands above your head. Do it right before you die. Thomas, I *have* to know."

The next morning, Thomas was tied to the stake and the fire was lit. The fire burned for a long time; most thought he was dead. Then, as the crowd watched, Thomas lifted his hands, "still on fire, over his head. He reached them up to the living God, and then, with great rejoicing, clapped them together three times."[7]

When I read that story, it makes me cry. Imagine being burned at the stake and raising your hands in worship to the living God. God's grace was sufficient for the apostle Paul and for Thomas Hauker. It will be sufficient for you.

His presence will be with you. Others may abandon you because you have rewritten your script. Jesus never will. He promises that His presence will be continually with you, even through persecution (see Hebrews 13:5). His Word tells us that "neither death nor life, neither angels nor demons, neither the present nor the future, nor any powers, neither height nor depth, nor anything else in all creation, will be able to separate us from the love of God" (Romans 8:38-39). If you cultivate an awareness of His presence now, you will experience it when the heat is on.

Your reward in heaven will be great. Jesus promised that those who are persecuted will receive a great reward in heaven (see Matthew 5:12). Revelation says that those who remain strong even through tribulation and persecution will be before the throne of God, serving Him day and night (see Revelation 7:15). I wonder, is this the reward Jesus was talking about? To be up close to the throne where God Himself sits, serving Him day and night? Could anything be better? There, face-to-face, we'll be able to see the sparkle in His eye and live forever in eternal joy with Him.

You Are the Sparkle in His Eye

As we close this chapter, may I remind you of something? You are the sparkle of God's eye. He is delighted in you. Maybe you were not made to feel you were the apple of anyone's eye when you were an infant. Maybe you were never the sparkle of anyone's eye growing up. It may feel even at this moment that many are frustrated with you because of the transformation happening in you. Take heart. Joy is still possible for you. It is within your reach, because you are the sparkle of Abba's eye. He loves you. He is very, very pleased with you. When you come into His presence, His eyes light up because you are His precious child. He has noticed how hard you have worked on rewriting your script. He's proud of you! Take a moment and talk with Abba. Reflect on His love. Can you see the sparkle in His eye?

PRAYING SCRIPTURE
TO INTERNALIZE TRUTH

"Praise and glory and wisdom and thanks and honor and power and strength be to our God for ever and ever" (Revelation 7:12). Holy One, Your Word tells me, "Salvation belongs to our God, who sits on the throne, and to the Lamb" (Revelation 7:10). Lord Jesus, You alone are worthy of all my praise because "with your blood you purchased men for God from every tribe and language and people and nation" (Revelation 5:9). Worthy are You, Lamb of God.

Lord, even though I am walking through very difficult circumstances, I want to rejoice. Teach me how to choose joy, knowing that these trials have come so that my faith—"of greater worth than gold, which perishes even though refined by fire—may be proved genuine and may result in praise, glory and honor when Jesus Christ is revealed" (1 Peter 1:6-7). Teach me to be patient until You come (see James 5:7). Teach me to "endure hardship as discipline" (Hebrews 12:7).

Since Christ suffered in His body, help me to arm myself with the same attitude He had. Teach me to live for the will of the Father (see 1 Peter 4:1-2). When I become weary, remind me to "fix [my] eyes on Jesus, the author and perfecter of [my] faith, who for the joy set before him endured the cross, scorning its shame, and sat down at the right hand of the throne of God" (Hebrews 12:2).

In every circumstance, Your grace is sufficient, Lord Jesus (see 2 Corinthians 12:9). Strengthen me with Your grace so that when the day of evil comes, I can stand firm. Help me to remember when I am insulted or persecuted for my faith that I have been given a platform for preaching the gospel. Remind me that I don't need to worry about what I'll say or how I'll say it. You have promised to provide the right words through Your Holy Spirit (see Matthew 10:17-20).

Lord Jesus, even if I am not suffering at this time, help me to remember and pray for those who are. Your Word tells me to remember those in prison as if I were their fellow prisoner, and those who are mistreated as if I myself were suffering (see Hebrews 13:3).

FURTHER TRANSFORMATION
Digging Deeper into the Scriptures

1. Meditate on and memorize James 1:2-3 as written here or in another translation.

   Consider it pure joy, my brothers, whenever you face trials of many kinds, because you know that the testing of your faith develops perseverance.

2. Read Philippians 4:4-8. List choices you can make to strengthen your joy center, based on these verses.

3. Read 1 Peter 1:3-7. How can the persecution we face birth in us a living hope? Why do you think God allows us to walk through the fires of persecution?

4. Read 2 Thessalonians 2:15. What challenge does Paul give to the believers in Thessalonica? What does it look like for you to stand strong regarding the rewriting you have done on your emotional script?

5. Read John 15:9-11. What key does Jesus give to His disciples about building their joy centers? What steps will you take this week to remain in Christ's love?

Probing Deeper into your Emotional Script

6. How would you define joy after reading this chapter? How has your definition of joy changed since reading this chapter?

7. Have you personally faced any persecution because of rewriting your emotional script? Journal about that in the space provided below.

8. Read Philippians 1:13. Paul looked for the blessing of being imprisoned. List in the space below specific ways God has blessed your life through the process of your rewriting your emotional script.

9. Read Philippians 2:13. What evidence do you have that God is at work in your life at this moment?

10. Read Philippians 3:13. What does it look like for you to forsake the old script and focus on the new script?

11. Read Philippians 4:13 and John 16:7. What do these verses say to you about the promised power of the Holy Spirit? How have you experienced His power recently in your life?

12. Unleash the power of praise. Get on your knees (if possible). Listen to worship music. Spend time praising God that you are the sparkle of His eye. Then write a prayer to Abba Father, telling Him how thankful you are to be the sparkle of His eye.

CHAPTER 10

LEAVE A GODLY LEGACY

You are the salt of the earth. . . .
You are the light of the world.

MATTHEW 5:13-14

Dear Becky,

If you are opening this letter, it's because you are sixty-five years old. Wow, that's a lot of years! It seems like a good time to do some serious reflecting. Remember the journey of rewriting your emotional script? Remember how the Holy Spirit enabled you to keep going, even when you felt like giving up? The redemptive work of God's grace in your life and the freedom you have experienced have been huge. But the choices you make from here on are equally important. Paul wrote, "It is for freedom that Christ has set us free. Stand firm, then, and do not let yourselves be burdened again by a yoke of slavery" (Galatians 5:1). Here are some questions you need to consider in light of this verse:

How are you doing at nurturing a desperate and determined

spirit toward God? Are you intentionally seeking Him above all else, or have you become lackadaisical in your pursuit of Him? Have you brought closure to the losses you have had to grieve?

What about control? Remember the commitment you made to surrender control daily? Have you regressed to old habits of manipulation? Would Steve, your children, sons and daughters-in-law, and grandchildren describe you as meek? How is your worry quotient? Are you experiencing freedom from fear? Are you more peaceful than you were ten or fifteen years ago? Have you become demanding or are you continuing to walk in meekness?

At one point in your life, you were so hungry for more of God and His righteousness in your life. You longed to be in His presence and to worship Him. You ate and drank in His Word as though you were starving and parched. You memorized Scripture. Is the same hunger still there? Have you cultivated your appetite or have you filled it with lesser things?

Would those closest to you describe you as merciful? Have the years made you more gracious or more intolerant? Have you become judgmental and critical? Do you gripe and complain about new worship styles or the way your kids are raising their kids? Will those who come after you remember you as merciful and gracious? Have you intentionally invested in your community? After you are gone, will anyone in your community miss you?

Long ago you committed to purity. David wrote, "Search me, O God, and know my heart. . . . See if there is any wicked way in me" (Psalm 139:23-24, NKJV). The ripple effect of sin is horrific. You know. You've experienced the horror firsthand. God says in Exodus 20:5 that the sins of the fathers are visited on their children. Consider carefully the choices you make daily so that your children and grandchildren will not have to clean up a mess after you're gone. Spend some time reflecting on these questions: Are you hiding anything? Are there any secrets that will be exposed after you are dead? Have you cultivated authentic and transparent relationships with others, modeling accountability?

How are your relationships? Are your relationships with Steve, your children, and grandchildren intact? If not, why not? Have you done everything humanly possible to be at peace with them? Have you withheld forgiveness or apologies from any family member or friend who has wronged you or whom you have wronged? Are you experiencing the freedom of your choices to forgive? Or have you allowed bitterness to creep back in? Bitterness means bondage. Don't go back. Instead, press on toward the goal, to be like Jesus.

Have you strengthened your joy center? Are you extolling the Lord at all times, even in the difficult times? Is His praise continually in your mouth? (see Psalm 34:1). Does your heart continually cry, "Holy"? Remember, He has created you to worship Him.

Jesus asked that you be salt and light in the world around you. When was the last time you shared Christ with anyone? How are you spending your time? Are you involved in deep life-giving relationships? Who are the women you are mentoring? Are you being faithful in their lives?

My beloved Lord Jesus, I now renew my commitment to You. You are King of kings and Lord of lords. Let me never forget the redemptive work You have done in my life. You are my Bridegroom and I adore You. You alone are my first love. May I praise and exalt You continually. Cleanse me from any old habits to which I have regressed. Help me to move forward from here, always teachable and willing to change and pursuing You intentionally. Strengthen my resolve to leave a godly legacy to those coming up behind me.

I've been thinking a lot about the kind of legacy I want to leave, and I wrote the above letter to remind myself about the revisions I've made to my emotional script and the kind of woman I want to become. Jesus said, "You are the salt of the earth," and "You are the light of the world. . . . Let your light shine before men, that they may see your good deeds and praise your Father in heaven" (Matthew 5:13,14,16). Salt makes a difference in your food. Light makes a difference in a dark surrounding. Jesus' desire is clear. He wants us to make a difference in the world in which we live. His desire is that we leave a legacy that is both godly and emotionally healthy, because we represent Him to the world around us.

My legacy is the fruit of the rewriting I have done. So is yours. For this reason it is imperative that you stand strong in the revisions you have made. Before I tell you how to stand strong, let's review the revisions we've made.

Review Your Revisions

If you regularly review the following revisions you've made, you'll be able to internalize them even more and ensure that you leave a godly legacy.

You considered your story. Even though you can't change your story, you looked at it honestly to identify what was written on your emotional script. You decided in your heart that you wanted to erase the old messages and embrace new attitudes. As a result, you committed to begin the journey.

You became desperate and determined for God. You recognized Christ as your only hope. You moved beyond pride and shame and cried out to Him for help.

You grieved your losses. You learned the language of lament and mourned your losses. You poured out your heart to the Lord and allowed the tears to flow. You experienced His comfort.

You let go of control. For some of you this was tough, but you did it and I am proud of you! You surrendered all control to God and submitted to His plans for your life. And you are faithfully working your demolition plan to destroy strongholds of control.

You set your appetite on God. You have been cultivating your appetite for God. As a result, you are experiencing the pleasure of His presence. There's nothing like it, huh? You've become intentional about seeking Him, praising Him, thinking about Him, singing to Him, and clinging to Him.

You extended mercy. You have put down your stones of judgment. You've learned to uproot the sinful attitudes preventing you from being merciful. You've asked for Christ's heart, allowed suffering and sorrow to soften your heart, engaged in small acts of mercy, and you've learned to hang with the hurting. As a result, you are feeling more compassionate.

You uprooted generational sin. You spent time reflecting (examining both your family tree and yourself), repenting (asking for godly sorrow over a particular sin and turning from that sin), and making restitution (apologizing and making amends to the people who have been hurt by your sin). You now have a plan that you have developed to deal with future temptation.

You forgave. By God's grace you have chosen to forgive. This was such a difficult choice, but you did it and God is so pleased! You admitted the truth, considered confronting, verbalized your forgiveness, moved beyond the role of a victim, celebrated closure, and now you are praying God's blessing for the very one who hurt you. As a result, you are experiencing peace beyond what you could have imagined. It's great, isn't it?

You have rewritten your definition of joy. You understand now that you are the sparkle of God's eye. You strengthen your joy center by looking for the blessing, recognizing God is at work in you, forsaking the old script, focusing on the new script, and remembering the promised power available to you. As a result, you are experiencing more joy than you ever thought possible.

If you have taken each of these steps the fruit of your choices will be a godly legacy! This is why it is so important for you to stick with your revisions! Don't second-guess the edits you have made on your emotional script. Instead, stand strong.

Make a Commitment to Stand Strong

In order to stand strong in my revisions and leave an emotionally healthy legacy, I have made the following five commitments. I encourage you to make them as well.

Commit to Authenticity, to Zero Tolerance for Secret Sins

Make a commitment to authenticity and truth telling. Live by this principle: "Confess your sins to each other and pray for each other so that you may be healed" (James 5:16). We were never meant to walk this road alone. God created and designed us for community, and if you want to be sure to stand by the revisions you have made to your emotional script, you must choose authenticity within the body of Christ. It's not an option; it's imperative!

That's why I have two mentors and two friends with whom I am completely honest. I have given them permission to ask me anything about my life and secret choices. They have earned that right by walking with me and faithfully loving me through the darkest hours of my life. I trust them and want to be an open book before them. They see the good, the bad, and the ugly, and yet they love me. Their love ensures that I don't go back to living from my old emotional script. They remind me of the revisions I have made — and I love them because they are honest with me.

If you are struggling with secret sins, if you have regressed to the old script, please be honest with someone who can help you: a godly counselor, a spiritual director, or a mature pastor. Don't leave a mess for your children to clean up after you've died. With the indwelling Christ you have the strength necessary to continue living life from your new script.

Commit to Giving Grace, to Zero Tolerance for a Judgmental Spirit or Bitterness

Grace should be the defining mark of every Christ follower. If you have completed the first nine steps of rewriting your emotional script, then you have begun to extend grace through avenues both of mercy and forgiveness. When we live in authentic community, we will have plenty of opportunities to practice grace giving.

Philip Yancey wrote about "breaking the cycle of un-grace."[1] It is all too common that bitterness, hatred, prejudice, and "un-grace" are passed down from one generation to the next. If you don't believe me, travel to Palestine. The bitterness between the Arabs and Israelis started way back in Genesis. Remember the story? God promised Sarah and Abraham a son. Sarah became impatient and gave her maid to Abraham, telling him to go to bed with her. (Oh, good plan, Sarah!) Ishmael was the son born out of that union. Then God fulfilled His promise by opening Sarah's womb, and Sarah gave birth to a son, Isaac. Sarah immediately realized she had made a terrible mistake by giving her servant to Abraham. And so the hostility began. That resentment has been passed down from generation to generation. As a result, the world keeps its eye on the Gaza Strip, waiting for an answer to the conflict. I wonder what would have happened if Abraham and Sarah had chosen to leave a legacy of grace?

We talked about the importance of uprooting generational sin in chapter 7. By committing to giving grace, you will be ensuring that you will not go back to generational patterns of bitterness and resentment.

Commit to Investing in Others, to Zero Tolerance for Indifference

Become involved in the lives of others through mentoring relationships, which are relationships in which you empower another by sharing your life experience and God-given resources.[2] Mentoring includes a rhythm of both encouraging and exhorting, with the goal of empowering someone to reach her God-given potential. I mentioned earlier that I have mentors. I also have several women whom I am mentoring. These relationships are invaluable in my life.

Mentoring has a ripple effect. As I submit to being mentored, I am then able to pour that encouragement and exhortation into the lives of those coming up behind me. Just as I have rewritten my script, I can come alongside other women and coach them as they rewrite their scripts. Mentoring isn't a new concept, by any means. Paul exhorted older women to train younger women "to love their husbands and children, to be self-controlled and pure" (Titus 2:3-5).

Recently, I was invited to a Legacy Tea for a well-loved Christian leader in our community. One hundred or more women gathered to honor Phyllis Stanley because of the godly influence she has had on so many. The women brought cards and letters expressing their thanks for the role Phyllis has played in their lives. Phyllis has taken the time to invest in many younger women. Her time and effort have resulted in a powerful, godly legacy.

Do you want to leave a godly legacy? Then commit to investing in others through mentoring relationships.

Commit to Saturating Your Mind with Scripture, to Zero Tolerance for Satan's Messages

We are called to be holy, just as God is holy (see 1 Peter 1:15). How is this even possible? The psalmist gave us the answer: "How can a young man [or woman] keep his way pure? By living according to your word." He went on, "I have hidden your word in my heart that I might not sin against you" (Psalm 119:9,11). Dear friend, if you don't saturate your mind with Scripture, it will automatically gravitate to your old script, because that's where it has become comfortable. It is the Holy Spirit's role to change you, but the more Scripture you memorize, the more you give Him to work with!

Dan Ball, one of my heroes, is one of the most godly men I know. When I'm with Dan I feel as if I have tasted a bit of heaven. He thinks like Jesus. When he prays I am left spellbound. I once asked him the secret to his astounding spiritual maturity. He told me that every day he memorizes and internalizes Scripture. His mind is so full of Scripture it has no room for Satan's messages. Dan says he has to continually review the verses he's memorized, or he will forget them.

What a legacy he is leaving his children and grandchildren! I've heard his granddaughters recite Scripture that their grandpop has taught them. I long to hand down that kind of legacy. Even as I write this, silently, I am recommitting to saturate my mind with Scripture.

Commit to Praise, to Zero Tolerance for Complaining

Become intentional about incorporating praise and thanksgiving into every day. I have repeated this many times throughout this book. If you want to stand strong in your new script, make it your goal to live a lifestyle of praise. Cultivate an attitude of thanksgiving. Be authentic with your feelings, but praise God anyway. The psalmist wrote, "Praise the Lord. How good it is to sing praises to our God, how pleasant and fitting to praise him!" (Psalm 147:1). Who do you want to be when you grow older? If you want to be pleasant, then start incorporating praise into every day, not just once a day but all day. The more you praise God, the less likely you will fall into habits of complaining.

Stormie Omartian has learned that praise is essential to rewriting your emotional script. She wrote,

> When you have been set free and are trying to rebuild your life in the Lord, the enemy will come and tell you, "You weren't really set free." "You're still the same old messed-up person you always were." "You haven't been transformed." "You'll never be any different." "It didn't happen." "Nothing ever breaks through for you." When you start hearing those kinds of messages, recognize where they are coming from and remember who it is who set you free. Say, "Lord, I lift up praise to you. I thank you for your promises to me. I praise you as my Deliverer. Thank you that you have set me free and will continue to set me free."[3]

Praising God transforms you. Praise results in gladness. The more you praise Him, the less you complain. The more you praise Him, the less you feel grumpy. The more you praise Him, the less you snap at others. The more you praise God for the transformation in your emotional script, the more you will see ongoing transformation. Start now, and watch what happens in your life. Future generations will remember you as someone who exuded worship and a grateful heart!

These five commitments reflect the kind of woman I want to be. I still have a long way to go. That can feel discouraging, because I so want the Holy Spirit to transform me. But when I get discouraged, I look back and remember how far I've come.

My New Emotional Script

My Old Emotional Script	My New Emotional Script
Shame	Dignity
Insecurity	Secure
Guilt	Freedom
Defensiveness	Nondefensive
Fear	Courageous
Driven	Less Driven
Anger	Forgiving
Worry	Peaceful
Mistrust	Trusting
Low Self-esteem	Healthy Self-Esteem
Control	Meek
Depressed	Joyful
Judgmental	Merciful

With the Holy Spirit's help I've done a lot of rewriting of my emotional script. Even though I continue to rewrite, I'm further along than I was a few years ago! There are times when God reveals a negative message I didn't know was there, and there are times when I slip back and react from the old messages. In those moments I remind myself that I don't have to live by that old script anymore. I have rewritten it! Those old, negative messages have been erased and rewritten with the truth of Scripture. As a result, I have embraced the attitudes outlined by Christ in the Beatitudes. My relationships are far deeper because I've got nothing to hide. I have more hope and joy because both those emotions are now centered in intimacy with Jesus Christ. No one can rob them from me.

The Lord has redeemed my "messy story." Oh, how I praise Him! He has bestowed on me "a crown of beauty instead of ashes, the oil of gladness instead of mourning, and a garment of praise instead of a spirit of despair" (Isaiah 61:3).

PRAYING SCRIPTURE
TO INTERNALIZE TRUTH

Lord God, I bow down and worship You. Someday I will gather around the throne with others. Faith will be sight. Day and night I will never stop saying, "Holy, holy, holy is the Lord God Almighty, who was, and is, and is to come. . . . You are worthy, [my Lord,] to receive glory and honor and power, for you created all things, and by your will they were created and have their being" (Revelation 4:8,11). Lamb of God, You are my redeemer. You have redeemed every part of my life. With Your blood You have purchased my freedom. You have taken the evil in my life and turned it around for good. I praise You that I have overcome the Evil One by the blood of the Lamb and the word of my testimony (see Revelation 12:11).

"You, O LORD, sit enthroned forever; your renown endures through all generations" (Psalm 102:12). Your dominion and power will endure through all generations (see Psalm 145:13). Father, as I think about the legacy I want to leave, I commit to You that I will declare Your name to my family. I will speak of Your faithfulness to my children and their children. Lord, I pray that my posterity will serve You; that future generations will be told about the Lord (see Psalm 22:30). May they proclaim Your righteousness—even those who are not yet born. I pray over them now that they will declare Your righteousness and that they will honor You with both their mouths and actions (see Psalm 22:23).

Holy Spirit, thank you for the transformation You've done in my emotional script. Help me not to return to old patterns of thought. Since I have been raised with Christ, teach me to set my heart on You (see Colossians 3:1). Lord, since I have taken off my old self with its practices, teach me not to lie but to practice truth telling in every area of my life. Help me not to fall back into old patterns of denial, but to stand strong in Your truth (see Colossians 3:9-10). Lord, thank you that I am Your chosen daughter, holy and dearly loved. Help me to clothe myself every day with compassion, kindness, humility, gentleness, and patience (see Colossians 3:12). Let my legacy reflect the peace of Christ. Show me how to let the Word of Christ dwell in my heart and mind (see Colossians 3:15-16). I know it is Your will for my mouth to be filled with Your praise and my heart to be filled with gratitude (Colossians 3:16). Let everything I do this day be for Your glory. May the legacy I leave reflect the glory of Your Son and my Savior, Jesus Christ.

FURTHER TRANSFORMATION
Digging Deeper into the Scriptures

1. Meditate on and memorize Matthew 5:16 as written here or in another translation.

   In the same way, let your light shine before men, that they may see your good deeds and praise your Father in heaven.

2. In your own words define *legacy*.

3. Read Matthew 5:13-16. What does it look like for you to be salt and light in your community? What do these verses say about the kind of legacy Christ wants us to leave?

4. Read John 15:5. How does rewriting your emotional script help you leave a more fruitful legacy?

5. Read Proverbs 31:10-31. This passage is an oracle, written to King Lemuel from his mother, describing the type of woman she believes would make her son a good wife. Sometimes this passage can feel terribly intimidating for women. But there are key elements in this oracle about how to leave a godly legacy. List the evidence that you can find in these verses of the type of legacy a virtuous woman can leave. To help you do this, I have divided the virtuous woman's sphere of influence into categories.

a. What kind of legacy does she leave her family?

b. What kind of legacy does she leave in her place of employment?

c. What kind of legacy does she leave in her community?

6. Read Ephesians 2:10 and James 2:26. What connection do you see between good works and a godly legacy? What good works do you think God has specifically prepared you to do?

7. Read 2 Timothy 1:5; 3:14-17. Describe the type of legacy that Timothy's mother and grandmother left to him.

Probing Deeper into Your Emotional Script

8. Someone has said, "Our stories are inextricably interwoven. What you do is a part of my story. What I do is a part of yours."[4] Think about this quote. How is this relevant to leaving a godly legacy? How might your story influence the next generation?

9. Write a description of your old emotional script, then write a description of your new emotional script. What changes have you experienced as a result of the rewriting you have done? How will these changes impact your legacy?

10. What qualities do you most want to be remembered for? How can you nurture those qualities now?

11. Write a letter to yourself that is similar to the one I wrote myself. Remind yourself of the type of woman you desire to be when you are sixty-five years old. (If you are sixty-five or older, write a letter to yourself describing who you want to be in the future and how you wish to be remembered.)

12. Unleash the power of praise. Read over the comparison of your old script versus your new script. Take a walk and praise the Holy Healer for every change you have seen in your life since doing this study.

NOTES

NOTE TO SMALL GROUP LEADERS

1. Adele Ahlberg Calhoun, *Spiritual Disciplines Handbook* (Downers Grove, IL: InterVarsity, 2005), 265.

CHAPTER 1

1. Dr. Chuck Lynch, *I Should Forgive, But . . .* (Nashville: Nelson, 1998), quoted in Beth Moore, *Praying God's Word* (Nashville: Broadman, Holman, 2000), 223.
2. Bill Hull, *Right Thinking* (Colorado Springs, CO: NavPress, 1985), 68.
3. Erwin Lutzer, foreword to *Lord, Change My Attitude*, by James MacDonald (Chicago: Moody, 2001), 10.

CHAPTER 2

1. Dorothy Kelley Patterson, *BeAttitudes for Women* (Nashville: Broadman, Holman, 2000), 24.
2. Rob Bell, *Velvet Elvis* (Grand Rapids, MI: Zondervan, 2005), 105.
3. Cynthia Spell Humbert, *Deceived by Shame, Desired by God* (Colorado Springs, CO: NavPress, 2001), 21.

CHAPTER 3

1. Stephen Arterburn, *Healing Is a Choice* (Nashville: Nelson, 2005), 74.
2. W. E. Vine, *An Expository Dictionary of New Testament Words* (Old Tappan, NJ: Revell, 1940), 87.
3. Philippians 4:4.
4. Jerry Sittser, *A Grace Disguised* (Grand Rapids, MI: Zondervan, 2005), 200.
5. Michael Card, *A Sacred Sorrow* (Colorado Springs, CO: NavPress, 2005), 11.

CHAPTER 4

1. W. E. Vine, *An Expository Dictionary of New Testament Words* (Old Tappan, NJ: Revell, 1966), 55.
2. Vine, 35.
3. Bruce B. Barton, Mark Fackler, Linda K. Taylor, and David R. Veerman, *Life Application Bible Commentary: Matthew* (Wheaton, IL: Tyndale, 1996), 77.
4. A. W. Tozer, *The Pursuit of God* (Camp Hill, PA: Christian Publications, 1982), 105.
5. Dorothy Kelley Patterson, ed., *The Woman's Study Bible* (Nashville: Nelson, 1995), 1978.
6. Vine, 239.
7. Vine, 238.
8. Beth Moore, *Praying God's Word* (Nashville: Broadman, Holman, 2000), 3.
9. Lisa Bevere, *Out of Control and Loving It!* (Lake Mary, FL: Creation House, 1996), 114.

CHAPTER 5

1. Bruce B. Barton, Mark Fackler, Linda K. Taylor, and David R. Veerman, *Life Application Bible Commentary* (Wheaton, IL: Tyndale, 1996), 78.
2. John MacArthur Jr., *The MacArthur New Testament Commentary:*

Matthew 1-7 (Winona Lake, IN: BMH Books, 1985), 181.

3. In the Greek these verbs are in the present continuous tense.
4. W. E. Vine, *An Expository Dictionary of New Testament Words* (Old Tappan, NJ: Revell, 1966), 298.
5. Dana Candler, *Deep unto Deep* (Kansas City, MO: Forerunner Publishing, 2004), 8.
6. A. W. Tozer, *The Pursuit of God* (Camp Hill, PA: Christian Publications, 1982), 20.

CHAPTER 6

1. W. E. Vine, *An Expository Dictionary of New Testament Words* (Old Tappan, NJ: Revell, 1940), 60.
2. Luke 5:17-26: Jesus healed the man who is paralyzed and forgives his sins; Luke 5:13: Jesus showed mercy to the leper; Luke 8:2: Jesus had mercy on Mary and cast out seven demons from her; Luke 18:35-42: Jesus gives mercy to the blind beggar.
3. Philip W. Comfort and Wendell C. Hawley, *Opening the Gospel of John* (Wheaton, IL: Tyndale, 1994), 345.
4. Dictionary.com, http://dictionary.com, s.v. "Indifference."
5. Becky Harling, "The Twenty-Minute Worship Challenge," *Discipleship Journal,* May/June 2007, 26.
6. Rolland and Heidi Baker, *Always Enough* (Grand Rapids, MI: Chosen Books, 2003), 164.

CHAPTER 7

1. W. E. Vine, *An Expository Dictionary of New Testament Words* (Old Tappan, NJ: Revell, 1940), 231.
2. M. Scott Peck, *People of the Lie: The Hope for Healing Human Evil* (New York: Simon & Shuster, 1983), 130.
3. Rose Marie Miller, *From Fear to Freedom* (Wheaton, IL: Harold Shaw Publishers, 1994), 42.
4. Vine, 279.
5. Becky Harling, *Finding Calm in Life's Chaos* (Colorado Springs, CO: NavPress, 2005), 138.

6. Vine, 280.
7. Beth Moore, *Praying God's Word* (Nashville: Broadman, Holman, 2000), 173.
8. See sidebar on page 153.

Chapter 8

1. W. E. Vine, *An Expository, Dictionary of New Testament Words* (Old Tappan, NJ: Revell, 1966), 170.
2. Vine, 260.
3. Vine, 170.
4. Sometimes it's not physically or emotionally safe to approach the other person about restoring the relationship. In such instances, being a peacemaker simply means forgiving that person.
5. R. T. Kendall, *Total Forgiveness* (Lake Mary, FL: Charisma House, 2002), 18.
6. James G. Friesen, E. James Wilder, Anne M. Bierling, Rick Koepcke, and Maribeth Poole, *Living from the Heart Jesus Gave You* (Van Nuys, CA: Shepherd's House, 2000), 47.
7. According to an article by Bessel van der Kolk, post-traumatic stress disorder occurs "when people become too upset by their emotions, [and] memories cannot be transmitted into a neutral narrative"; see "Posttraumatic Stress Disorder and Memory," *Psychiatric Times,* March 1997, http://www.psychiatrictimes.com/p970354.html.
8. Luke 5:20, nkjv; Luke 7:48, nkjv.
9. Spiros Zodhiates, ed., *The Complete Word Study Dictionary: New Testament* (Iowa Falls, IA: World Bible Publishers, 1992), #863.
10. Beth Moore, *Praying God's Word* (Nashville: Broadman, Holman, 2000), 221.
11. Kate Naseef, "How Can the Amish Forgive What Seems Unforgivable?" *USA Today,* October 2, 2007.
12. Dictionary.com, http://dictionary.com, s.v. "Excruciating."
13. Jane Rubietta, *Quiet Places* (Minneapolis: Bethany, 1997), 78.
14. Susan Lee, *The Dancer* (Grand Rapids, MI: Baker, 1991), 54.

15. Philip Yancey, *What's So Amazing About Grace?* (Grand Rapids, MI: Zondervan, 1997), 83.

16. Kathy Olsen, *Silent Pain* (Colorado Springs, CO: NavPress, 1992), 17.

17. Robert S. McGee and William Drew Mountcastle, *Conquering Eating Disorders* (Nashville: LifeWay Press, 1993), 172.

CHAPTER 9

1. Dorothy Kelley Patterson, *BeAttitudes for Women* (Nashville: Broadman, Holman, 2000), 233.

2. Patterson, 230.

3. Dictionary.com, http://dictionary.com, s.v. "Joy."

4. James G. Friesen, E. James Wilder, Anne M. Bierling, Rick Koepcke, and Maribeth Poole, *Living from the Heart Jesus Gave You* (Van Nuys, CA: Shepherd's House, 2000), 12.

5. Friesen et al., 11.

6. About.com:Biology, "Regeneration of Brain Cells," http://biology.about.com/library/weekly/aa102199.htm.

7. DC Talk and Voice of the Martyrs, *Jesus Freaks* (Tulsa, OK: Albury Publishing), 144.

CHAPTER 10

1. Philip Yancey, *What's So Amazing About Grace?* (Grand Rapids, MI: Zondervan, 1997), 65.

2. Adele Ahlberg Calhoun, *Spiritual Disciplines Handbook* (Downers Grove, IL: InterVarsity, 2005), 141.

3. Stormie Omartian, *The Prayer That Changes Everything* (Eugene, OR: Harvest House, 2005), 263.

4. Daniel Taylor, "In Pursuit of Character, Part 2," *Christianity Today,* http://www.christianitytoday.com/ct/1995/december11/5te29b.html?start=4.

ABOUT THE AUTHOR

B ECKY HARLING is a frequent speaker at women's conferences and retreats nationally as well as internationally. She is the author of *Finding Calm in Life's Chaos*. Drawing from her experience as a pastor's wife, mother, and breast cancer survivor, Becky delivers a message of hope and healing to women that is refreshingly transparent. Her husband, Steve, is the lead pastor at Foothills Community Church in Arvada, Colorado. Steve and Becky have four grown children. To schedule Becky for your event and to learn more about her ministry, visit www.beckyharling.com.

Can't get enough? Check out these other great titles from NavPress!

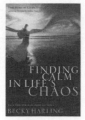

Finding Calm in Life's Chaos
Becky Harling
978-1-57683-619-4

Becky Harling, cancer survivor, shares personal insight in this women's Bible study for finding calm amidst whatever life may bring by looking at Jesus' "I Am" statements. Discover a fresh understanding of who God is through these "I Am" statements. Each chapter includes Bible study questions and exercises designed to help women step out of the busyness of life and find rest in God.

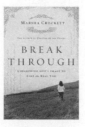

Break Through
Marsha Crockett
978-1-60006-185-1

Marsha Crockett knows the pain of a hard life. She invites you to search for the promise of God's power as you reconcile the reality of life with your faith. Through journal suggestions, Scripture meditation exercises, and practical tips, you'll learn how to move from stone-like hardness into a place of grace and truth.

Satisfy My Thirsty Soul
Linda Dillow
978-1-57683-390-2

As a Christian woman, you yearn for intimacy with God. You long to know His presence, to be satisfied in heart and soul, but you don't know how. You want to be obedient, but you need a higher motivation than simply choosing to do right. Linda Dillow understands. And now in *Satisfy My Thirsty Soul*, she shares with you her lifelong discovery that both longings can be met—through worship.

To order copies, call NavPress at 1-800-366-7788 or log on to www.navpress.com.